MARCO

LAKE GAR DA

GERMANY
Stuttgart   Munich

FRA.

Bern   AUSTRIA
SWITZERLAND   Bolzano

Lake Garda   SLOVENIA
Milan   Trieste
    Verona   CROATIA
      Venice

Genoa   ITALY   Adriatic
     San Marino   Sea
Ligurian   Florence
Sea

FREE!

THE TOURING APP

shows you the way...
including routes and offline maps!

GET MORE OUT OF YOUR MARCO POLO GUIDE

IT'S AS SIMPLE AS THIS

1 go.marco-polo.com/gar

2 download and discover

GO!

WORKS OFFLINE!

SYMBOLS

INSIDER TIP	Insider-Tip
★	Highlight
●●●●	Best of ...
☼	Scenic view
✪	Responsible travel: for ecological or fair trade aspects
(*)	Telephone numbers that are not toll-free

PRICE CATEGORIES HOTELS

Expensive	over 120 euros
Moderate	80–120 euros
Budget	under 80 euros

Prices per night for two persons in double room including breakfast in low season

PRICE CATEGORIES RESTAURANTS

Expensive	over 35 euros
Moderate	25–35 euros
Budget	under 25 euros

Prices for a meal with starter, main course and a drink

CONTENTS

DID YOU KNOW?
Timeline → p. 14
For bookworms → p. 24
Local specialities → p. 28
Public holidays → p. 121
Budgeting → p. 127
Weather → p. 128
Currency converter → p. 129

MAPS IN THE GUIDEBOOK
(136 A1) Page numbers and coordinates refer to the road atlas
(0) Site/address located off the map

Coordinates are also given for places that are not marked on the road atlas

(𝄐 A–B 2–3) refers to the removable pull-out map

INSIDE FRONT COVER:
The best highlights

INSIDE BACK COVER:
Street maps of Bardolino, Riva, Salò and Sirmione

The best MARCO POLO Insider Tips

Our top 15 Insider Tips

INSIDER TIP **Freshly caught whitefish**

The locals are happy to queue: Alberto Rania is one of about 50 fishermen working every day to catch sardines and whitefish from the *lago.* He sells the day's fresh catch or fish preserved in salt and oil three times a week at the Piazza in Riva → p. 23

INSIDER TIP **German-style beer garden**

Instead of sitting under chestnut trees as you would in Germany, locals as well as holidaymakers relax in the shade of olive trees at the *Speckstube* in Malcesine. Enjoy traditional German dishes such as a ham hock, ribs and a cool beer in peace and watch the kids tumble about the playground on the large meadows → p. 37

INSIDER TIP **Tempt your taste buds!**

Those who enjoy the taste of Trentino cuisine can join a *tasting session* in what used to be an aristocratic Palazzo Roccabruna in the heart of Trento → p. 29

INSIDER TIP **Aperitif in the oil mill**

Every Tuesday evening, the oil mill of *Azienda Agricola Manestrini* near Manerba offers tours combined with a tasting of olive oil, wines and other typical local products → p. 95

INSIDER TIP **Historic and culinary heights**

Within the walls of the *Azienda Agricola Pratello*, you can eat and sleep like a medieval guest in modern comfort. The vineyard specializes in organic wines → p. 75

INSIDER TIP **Caribbean feeling**

Giamaica Beach near Sirmione certainly lives up to its name: hot springs and turquoise blue water → p. 78

INSIDER TIP **Soooo romantic**

Romantic and organic: on a moonlit night, *wine tasting* at the *Villa Calicantus* in the hills of Bardolino is even more delightful → p. 53

BEST OF ...

FOR FREE

● *Curiosities and culture*

Is it the shortest river in the world? The source of the Aril River is in Cassone near Malcesine and it flows into the lake after a leisurely 175 m/574 ft. In Cassone harbour there is the small, carefully curated fishing museum *Museo del Lago.* Admission free! → p. 39

● *Card with discounts!*

With the free *Garda Promotions Card* you receive discounts for numerous attractions like amusement parks, museums and ferry rides. It is available free of charge at your accommodation or from Tourist Information Offices. → p. 127

● *Jazz for free*

The *jazz cafés'* concerts in June and July are all free of charge → p. 38

● *Aperitif with snacks*

With a fizzy drink – spritz (photo) – or a glass of Spumante in your hand, you can end the day in true Italian style. The best place to go is one of the classic aperitif bars that offer delicious and filling snacks for free with an aperitif, such as the *Riva Bar* in the town of the same name → p. 43

● *Terrace of the thrill*

The impressive mountain scenery rises high above the lake at the north-western shore. Those who want to enjoy this amazing panoramic view should travel to Tremosine. In Pieve, stand on this *"Terrace of the thrill"* at the Hotel Paradiso and gaze into the depths. You can then order a cappuccino and relax → p. 90

● *Church concerts*

The acoustics are particularly good: classical *concerts* are held on Wednesdays in summer in San Nicolò Church in Bardolino. Listening to the music is a delightful experience – and a free one! → p. 54

●●●● Dots in guidebook refer to "Best of..." tips

● *A beauty pageant for castles*
The powerful Scaliger family of Verona ruled over the east shore for centuries. In the 13th and 14th centuries they built *castles* as a sign of their strength: in Malcesine (photo), in Torri del Benaco and in Sirmione. Find out for yourself which is the most beautiful! → p. 36, 67, 76

● *Fish from the lake*
Some 50 professional fishermen on the lake catch what both visitors and locals like to eat: whitefish, trout and the rare Lake Garda trout called *carpione*. The day's catch is sold at the fish cooperative market *Cooperativa Fra Pescatori* in Garda → p. 58

● *A glass of Bardolino*
The vineyards that produce the Bardolino wine are on the slopes above the village of the same name. You can sample and buy wine directly from the producers, e.g. at *Cantine Lenotti* → p. 54

● *Take to the water!*
Just how beautifully the villages snuggle into the hills along the lakeside can best be seen from the water. And whoever wants to explore the opposite side of the lake can simply take *a ferry between Torri and Toscolano* → p. 127

● *Mountain paradise for the very active*
Many outdoor enthusiasts, who travel to Lake Garda, can be found on *Monte Baldo* – either racing downhill on bikes, hiking to the summit or skiing down the slopes → p. 40, 113

● *Seductive plant world*
The aromatic fragrance of lemon trees, bougainvillea and rosemary is all-pervasive. In many garden centres, e.g. the *Flover* in Bussolengo, there are occasionally small trees, which you can take home in your car → p. 64

● *Alpine sensation with a Mediterranean touch*
You can do this between Riva and Torbole, e.g. at the *Bar alla Sega*: enjoy sitting beneath the palms and oleander trees and sip a cappuccino or aperitif, while you gaze at the deep blue lake and appreciate the wonderful backdrop of the 2000 m/6562 ft mountains → p. 46

ONLY IN

BEST OF ...

● *The path of the water*
At *Sea Life Gardaland*, visitors can trace the course of the water from a mountain stream through Lake Garda and the Po River delta to the Mediterranean Sea and the ocean. Sea horses swim alongside corals and sharks in the aquarium → p. 119

● *City trip*
There are three ways to keep out of the rain on a visit to nearby *Verona*: visit one of its many museums, its famous churches such as San Zeno, and all sorts of inviting shops. You can drift from one boutique to the next along the Via Mazzini → p. 65

● *That's cheese!*
It's true! The *Alpe del Garda* cheese dairy in Tremosine produces plenty of cheese. Those who are interested can join a tour and, on request, also a cheese tasting. Yummy! → p. 90

● *Bouldering under a roof*
When it rains, climbers can still get their adrenaline kick at *Bouldercity* in Pietramurata. The bouldering centre has 7000 ft² climbing walls that are up to 5 m/16.4 ft high and over 200 routes so there is always something for everyone → p. 113

● *Varone waterfall*
It makes no real difference what the weather is doing: the *Cascata del Varone* created by the Tenno stream sends a veil of spray into this narrow gorge (photo). "A hellish spectacle" noted Thomas Mann (photo) → p. 44

● *A visit to the wine museum*
The ideal place to learn about wine and try a drop or two is the *Museo del Vino* of the Cantina Zeni in Bardolino. It offers a glimpse into the many facets of growing wine in the Verona region. Visitors can learn about everything from the cultivation of the vines to the filling of the bottles → p. 52

RAIN

RELAX AND CHILL OUT
Take it easy and spoil yourself

● *Find your inner peace*

Many hotels on the lake offer yoga and meditation courses for stressed holidaymakers. In the Buddhist centre *Kushi Ling* above Arco, however, this kind of relaxation is a way of life and not just a trend → **p. 49**

● *Farm holidays*

Is the hustle and bustle on the shores a bit too much for you? Then check out the fully renovated *Antica Cascina Liano* situated high above Gargnano in the green countryside of the Parco Alto Garda that was once a farm, but now offers peace and quiet with a rustic ambiance – and a broad view of the lake → **p. 88**

● *A cappuccino with a touch of fun*

While the kids explore the *Busatte Parco Avventura* high above Torbole with its high ropes course, BMX track and football field on a large meadow, parents can enjoy a cappuccino on the terrace of the adjacent restaurant and watch the fun from afar → **p. 46**

● *An open-air bathtub*

The water in *Parco Termale del Garda* has a temperature of 37 °C/98.6 °F. Relax and unwind in this park with its thermal lake encircled by old trees, which is also open in the evenings → **p. 64**

● *An oasis of harmony*

In the large spa at *Lefay Resort & Spa* (photo) in Gargnano, the Orient meets the Occident in an oasis of wellness that is also environmentally conscious → **p. 88**

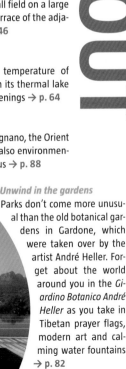

● *Unwind in the gardens*

Parks don't come more unusual than the old botanical gardens in Gardone, which were taken over by the artist André Heller. Forget about the world around you in the *Giardino Botanico André Heller* as you take in Tibetan prayer flags, modern art and calming water fountains → **p. 82**

11

INTRODUCTION

DISCOVER LAKE GARDA!

Lake Garda has myriad attractions – and all fans will discover some aspect of its unique charm. It certainly has broad appeal and offers guests *a taste of the Mediterranean lifestyle*. For those living in central Europe, it is the nearest place to the *dolce vita*.

Those who have once been spellbound by the *lago* will return time and again. Why? Is that because of the wonderful *centri storici*, the palms, the cypress trees or olive groves? Or are the many castles, *medieval villages* or picturesque harbours the main attractions? Or is it perhaps the crispy pizzas, fruity ice cream and quaffable red wine? It's most likely because *we feel at home here*. Lago di Garda is the "southernmost lake of Munich" and its dimensions 143 mi2 (exactly twice the size of the Fehmarn island, off the German and Danish coast) satisfies cravings for a seaside holiday. Well, almost: at its widest point, the lake measures 17 km/10.6 mi ... Those who plan to rapidly explore its many aspects can drive around the lake in four to five hours – yet only during low season. The Gardesana is a narrow and curvy road, and during the summer it is often congested with traffic.

Simple Trentino cuisine is served up at La Montanara on a side street in the old town centre of Riva

The northern side of the lake is quite different from the south, and the same goes for the east and western shores. These contrasts give the lake its special charm. Half way down the western shore it is extremely peaceful. For those of you who are content to read the newspaper or a book and are happy to hear nothing other than the flapping of *sails in the wind* and the sound of moored boats clanging together, Gargnano is the place for you. *Classy hotels* are traditional in this part of the lake. In the late 19th century, German hotelier Louis Wimmer already recognized the charm of Lake Garda and built the first grand hotel, in Gardone. Others soon followed. Here, rather old-fashioned, respectable tourism still prevails.

On the other hand, the eastern shore has a *younger vibe and is livelier* – but is just as picturesque. If you like shopping and want people around you until late,

From 2000 BC
Celts, Raetians and Venetians settle in the Lake Garda area

15 BC
The Romans arrive at the lake and name it "Benacus"

9th/10th centuries
Carolingian emperors and kings, as well as local princes, fight for supremacy in Upper Italy

1260–1387
The Scaligers rule in and around Verona

1387–1405
The Milanese Visconti family rules over the Lake Garda area

Bardolino and Garda will suit you. The little lanes of the Old Towns are almost more crowded in the evenings than during the day, and you see children running around with ice creams in their hands until midnight. If you're up for a *real taste of nightlife*, then head to the south shore. Some of the biggest discos in and around Desenzano are popular with disco fans from the region.

The mountains and winds form a grand divide from north to south. The fjord-like north with up to 2000 m/6562 ft high mountains offers every keen *outdoor sportsman and sportswoman* the perfect conditions: adventure-lovers can try their luck canyoning and explore otherwise inaccessible ravines accompanied by mountain guides. Mountain bikers and hikers roam the mountain slopes. Where it gets too steep for them, climbers ascend the rugged rock faces and are sometimes suspended directly over the lake. For landlubbers, the terrain gets tough. But not for water sports fans, as Lake Garda's *constant winds,* the *ora* and *pelér*, between Limone, Riva del Garda and Malcesine, make this one of Europe's ideal locations for sailing. Sometimes, however, the *lake traffic* can get out of hand. 50

> It's extremely peaceful half way down the western shore

years ago, mainly surfers and sailors floated across the waves, whereas the lake is now popular with kitesurfers, stand-up paddlers and kayakers. Water-skiing and parasailing are also popular, although mainly in the south, as motorboats are not allowed in the north.

1405–1797
The Venetians take control of the east shore

1797
The west shore is taken over by Napoleon's Cisalpine Republic; Austria is given the east shore and Verona

1814/15
After Napoleon's overthrow, the Congress of Vienna grants Austria Lombardy and the Veneto

1821–1861
Risorgimento period, the movement for Italian unification. Italy becomes a sovereign state in 1861

1919
After World War I, the lake is now completely Italian

Basically, the further south you travel, the more crowded things get, especially during the hot summer months. The beaches are full and it is difficult to find parking spaces. It's not surprising because the shoreline is wider, and occasionally even with a sandy beach like at Spiaggia d'Oro in Lazise.

However, don't worry that it will be too busy during the summer. Even during the peak season you will find *quiet places to retreat*, it's just knowing where to look. You can enjoy watching the sunset at a *picturesque jetty in the harbour*, for instance, in Cassone near Malcesine, and ignore the hubbub with an aperitif in your hand and a view of the lake. Or you can explore the area behind the lake. Even regular holiday-makers on Lake Garda frequently discover new and exciting places for excursions.

Authentic cuisine with local products

What about the food? No matter which holiday resort you have chosen, the food is excellent even in very touristy places. That applies regardless of whether you choose a pizza, pasta, risotto or polenta dish, order a lavish three-course meal in a gourmet restaurant in Salò or a simple *grilled Lake Garda trout*. The chefs in the region are increasingly offering authentic cuisine featuring local products and specialities. That also goes for the wine. Whereas in the past, holidaymakers still used to buy cheap wine in large bottles in wicker holders, the demand is now for fine quality. Whatever your taste in wine, whether you enjoy fruity and light or dry and spicy, Lake Garda is a wine-growing area for different *wine varieties*. In the north, the red, full-bodied Marzemino goes well with hearty fare, wine lovers in the south prefer to drink a well-chilled rosé Bardolino Chiaretto with fish dishes.

Lake Garda is not just a paradise for adventurous sports fans, sun worshippers searching for relaxation and connoisseurs looking forward to making new discoveries. Famous guests like Goethe, Nietzsche or Kafka once hunted for art treasures here. Today, culture lovers will also find *a variety of cultural destinations*. For example, the harmonious Romanesque church of San Severo in Bardolino or the Roman villa Grotte di Catullo in Sirmione. If you enjoy short excursions, you can also admire the Piazza Duomo in Trento or stroll through Verona and visit the Roman Arena. A particularly enjoyable alternative when looking for attractions is a kayak or *canoe tour along*

1943–45
The Republic of Salò is formed under the rule of the fascist dictator Benito Mussolini towards the end of World War II

1946
After a referendum, Italy becomes a republic

1962
The cable car from Malcesine to the top of Monte Baldo is opened

2013
The MuSe, Italy's largest museum of natural sciences, opens in Trento

2015
The region presents itself by sponsoring many events at the Expo in Milan

Lake Garda's shore: villas, which are not visible from the roadside, are revealed in all their splendour and the yellow fruits are a beautiful feature of the old lemon groves. An ideal starting point for *sightseeing tours on the water* is Gargnano, an attractive resort on the western shore, where many centuries ago wealthy owners once built their majestic villas.

Lemon delight: In, around and about Limone the yellow lemon fruits thrive

Nowadays, life on the lake is largely governed by tourism. It is of course not just those directly affected by the streams of tourists (hoteliers and restaurateurs, for example) who make a living from them. Fruit vendors selling at market stalls, craftsmen renovating holiday homes, Lake Garda fishermen supplying the trattorias, and *cheese-producing dairy farmers* up in the mountains. Unfortunately, tour-

> **The yellow fruits are a beautiful feature of the old lemon groves**

ism isn't only a blessing for the region. The heavy traffic, in particular, is a problem. A good tip: avoid using the car as much as possible when holidaying on the lake!

Yet despite the strong concentration on tourism, at Lake Garda you don't need to worry about being ripped off as a holidaymaker. Italians appreciate tourists and you are treated very civilly in tourist offices and restaurants, as if you have been a regular visitor for years. Happy holidays!

WHAT'S HOT

1 Green vineyards

Organic-issimo Young wine-growers go green. The ⓦ *Cantina della Valtenesi e della Lugana (www.civielle.com)* in Moniga del Garda produces wines with names such as "Biocora – the dance of life". There is also an organic Bardolino, including the prize-winning ⓦ *Cantina di Custoza (www.cantinadicustoza.it)*. The Azienda Agricola ⓦ *Le Sincette (www.lesincette.it)* in Picedo di Polpenazze presses wine and olive oil according to the guidelines of the organic certifier Demeter.

Fun for the kids

2

Making life easier for parents Italians love children and they know that offering the kids a playground at a restaurant works wonders for the parents' relaxation. Around the lake there are more and more restaurants with bouncy castles in the gardens, like at *La Cantinota (www.lacantinota.it)* in Arco where there are play areas on the meadows, or at the *Agriturismo Le Caldane (www.agriturismolecaldane.com)* in Lazise, or even a children's zoo like at *La Fattoria* (see p. 42) in Riva.

3 Sushi by the lake

Maki meets Mascarpone Food goes global: the craze for sushi has even reached Lake Garda, although it's already popular elsewhere. You can try the *Sushi Club* in Desenzano, *Lakhu (www.lakhu.it)* in Sirmione or *Sushoku* in Riva. The Italians also love indulging their taste for this classic Japanese food. However, Italian sushi has a Mediterranean twist – Uramaki with Mozzarella, tomatoes and basil (an "Italian roll") is just as essential as Temaki stuffed with Mascarpone.

Organic lifestyle

Organics as a mark of distinction Alternative food and lifestyles are now also a social statement in Northern Italy, although here things tend to be glamorous. Despite the amazing pric-es, the health food craze has also reached the shores of Lake Garda. There are more and more wholefood supermarkets, e.g. ⊗ *Mondo Vegan (Viale Tommaso dal Molin 16)* in Desenzano, and vegetari-an restaurants like ⊗ *Bio Essere Risto & Caffè (Via Santa Caterina 40 | www. bioesserearco.com)* in Arco. Many ice cream parlours also label their ve-gan ice cream flavours. Almost every small village also has an *erboristeria,* a health food store that resembles a phar-macy. Whether you're looking for calendu-la cream or throat sweets: here, you will find plenty of herbal remedy products – and some ex-cellent and friendly advice.

Craft beer

Cheers! Those who think that the hillsides and slopes around Lake Garda are only a source for first-class wines such as Lugana, Marzemino or Nosiola are wrong: a while ago, the bar tenders only offered Belgian or German beer but more often than not local craft beer now fills the glasses. In numerous villages, tasty craft beers are produced by small breweries or *micro birrerie,* including specialities such as chestnut beer, or beer matured in oak barrels or even beer containing grape juice. One of the first to open on the lake was the *Manerba Brewery (www.manerbabrewery.it)* in Manerba. In the Val di Ledro you can find un-filtered beer that only contains fresh mountain water *(www.birrificioleder.it).*

IN A NUTSHELL

N AKED OR NOT NAKED?

Sauna culture in northern and southern climates tends to clash, especially when it's a question of going naked or not. It's no different on Lake Garda. Older generations of Italians wouldn't dream of going naked in public, and that's still true for young people even at public swimming pools or on the beach. Meanwhile, more and more public saunas display signs which suggest that it is healthier not to wear bathing costumes in the sauna. This is not to say that Italians will have a change of heart.

F LAVOURSOME GOLDEN THREADS

Lake Garda is well known as the source of many special culinary ingredients, especially olive oil and wine. However, a little-known fact is that it is also the source of an Oriental ingredient: saffron, a variety of crocus with fragrant threads grows around the lake. The locals use the precious spice not only to flavour their *risotto alla milanese,* but also to season numerous regional specialities like the crust on the Alpine cheese tombea and the crunchy *torta sbrisolona,* the traditional tart from the southern end of Lake Garda. In some places, even mashed potato is coloured golden yellow. The saffron is mainly cultivated at the feet of Monte Baldo, in Pravelle, in Gargnano and in Val di Ledro. In Pozzolengo, at the ⊙ INSIDERTIP *Azienda Agricola Al Muràs (www.zafferanodipozzolengo.it)*

Bathing fun in January, oil for the hair and skin and flower threads worth their weight in gold: Fun facts and an A–Z of the lake

fine quality organic saffron has been successfully cultivated – every year about 3 kg/6.6 lb of saffron is produced. In other words, approximately 600,000 saffron flowers are harvested by hand and partly immediately processed into fine delicacies. Do you want to try some? Then, it's well worth a visit to the farm's store!

ᛁCY DIP AND TRADITION

Have you ever been cold? *Ice*-cold?! No? Then, visit Riva del Garda on New Year's Day. Plenty of people living close to Lake Garda welcome in the new year with a proverbial dip in the ice-chilled water. For the past 20 years, on New Year's Day from 11am about 100 daredevil swimmers arrive to swim in temperatures around zero and to join in the *Tuffo di Capodanno*. Everybody wears bathing suits and waits for the starting pistol on the main piazza before swimming once around the harbour. All age groups join in – from ten-year-olds to healthy retirees. You can watch the event on *short. travel/gar22*! In Pieve, at Lake Ledro, they wait until the end of the month: according to legend, the three coldest days of the year are about now – so-called *giorni della merla*, or "days of the Merla (blackbird hen)". This is why the traditional dip in the Ledro is known as the *Tuffo della Merla:* since 2008, about 80 participants take the plunge into the icy waters of Lake Ledro.

TUNNELS AND AMAZING PANORAMIC VIEWS

Expletives can be heard from many a car driver: 30 km/h (19 mph) speed restrictions along the stretch of road from Riva del Garda to Gargnano and 74 tunnels. Some are so narrow that two motorhomes can only just pass and if there is a group of cyclists then... The Gardesana Occidentale, however, is considered one of the most beautiful roads in Italy. And wherever openings in tunnels and galleries reveal glimpses of the lake, then you'll realise why. It was built after World War I, not for tourists, but to link the north of the lake – which at that time became part of Italy – to the south. The slightly wider and not quite so spectacular Gardesana Orientale runs along the opposite bank. As the old roads cannot cope with today's amount of traffic at all, both routes are closed to lorries in the summer.

WINTER ON THE LAKE

Admit it, you've never thought of spending winter on Lake Garda. That's a mistake! Winter is the most relaxed season and the time when locals take their bikes out of the cellar and parking meters are covered in plastic film. Of course, not all the shops and bars are open and many of the hotels are shut – but that's more than made up for by the peace and quiet everywhere. The best thing is the weather. Unlike in summer, the mist rarely descends, but the days are clear and the sky is blue. Then there's the deep blue water of the lake, the green palms and olive trees and the white mountain summits in the north. If you are protected from the wind you can remove your pullover, and enjoy the sunshine. Then, there is a wide variety of winter sports! Theoretically, you can enjoy a skiing tour one day on Monte Stivo and go ice climbing the next day, while on the third day you can climb in Massone – in a T-shirt, if you are lucky. On Monte Baldo there is even a small skiing area. The real surprise is the Christmas season: Christmas Markets have recently become popular, especially with the residents. In Riva, Bardolino, Garda or Tremosine – the Christmas lights twinkle everywhere

and seasonal treats, toys and handcrafted souvenirs are available to purchase at the wooden stalls. Many of the markets are open until early January.

WHATSAPP UPDATES FROM FISHERMEN

When Alberto Rania arrives at Piazza Battisti in Riva around 10am, the locals are already standing in a queue. They are all waiting for him to open his three-wheeler "Ape", which has been converted to a refrigerated transporter, to reveal the shiny fish on ice. About 40 different fish varieties live in Lake Garda. There are many local varieties as well as several that have accidentally arrived in the lake from the surrounding rivers, while others were deliberately introduced. Al-

berto is among the last 50 professional fishermen on Lake Garda. Most of them have joined cooperatives that manage the sale and processing of the fish. For example, the Cooperativa Pescatori in Garda where the day's fresh catch is auctioned. Alberto is self-employed and he sells the INSIDER TIP day's fresh fish every Tuesday, Friday and Saturday from 10am to 12noon in front of the castle in Riva. Regular customers receive WhatsApp updates about the day's catch. The fish are then cleaned and set aside. Anyone who is interested can also receive helpful cooking tips. *www.albertorania.it*

TREASURE FROM MONTE BALDO

The truffle (or *tartufo* in Italian) is a fungus – but what a misnomer for such an

Wonderfully romantic and still an insider tip: the Christmas season on the Lago

exquisite culinary delight! They grow underground among the roots of deciduous trees. Regions in this guide known for their truffles are Monte Baldo on the eastern shore and Parco Alto Garda Bresciano on the western side of Lake Garda. In autumn, Tignale hosts the truffle festival Sagra del Tartufo *(www.tignale.org)*. Pigs were traditionally used to snuffle out truffles which they reliably found – but were only too eager to gobble up themselves. Nowadays dogs are used instead. Hunting for truffles in restricted by law: only official *tartufari* are allowed to dig for the expensive tubers. Private individuals looking for truffles can be fined for poaching!

SOUR IS REJUVENATING

Alberto Dagnoli is proud of this: he is over 70 years old and healthy. His secret: plenty of fresh fish, olive oil and of course lemons. The pensioner is a tourist guide and is passionate about accompanying all those who are interested through the lemon groves in Limone. He knows the inhabitants of Limone live longer. The best example is his grandparents who also helped well into their old age. Why do the *Limonesi* enjoy particularly long lives? It has less to do with the diet of the residents in this formerly isolated fishing village – this mainly comprises fish, olive oil and lemons. Instead, it is because of a genetic mutation that applies to about 40 residents in the village. This helps to concentrate cholesterol in the blood and to transport it to the liver, so preventing cardiovascular disease. Alberto's brother is among one of the lucky ones (unlike Alberto). Never mind, Alberto feels fit and healthy and he swears by his daily intake of sour citrus fruits!

OIL FOR CONNOISSEURS

Lake Garda without olive oil? That would be like Munich without the beer! Ivo Bertamini laughs. He is an olive-grower in the north of Lake Garda and for about the last 50 years he has managed a traditional olive oil press or *frantoio* near Arco *(www.gardatrentino.it/de/frantoio bertamini)*. "We press the olives with a real mill stone. Compared with the oils from technology-operated mills, our oil tastes softer and less spicy." For several years, he has also been producing INSIDER TIP cosmetic products like soap, shampoo and creams. However, on the numerous terraces and gardens around the lake, olive trees are not only cultivated as a main occupation. Many families have several trees and produce their own oil. This is labour-intensive work. Not many people who dress their salad with olive oil from Lake Garda realize that all the olives here are harvested by hand. One tree yields about

FOR BOOK-WORMS

Twilight in Italy – in 1912 the English writer D. H. Lawrence hiked across the Alps to Italy and stayed in Gargnano with his lover. In this work he describes the days he spent on Lake Garda

111 Places in Verona and Lake Garda That You Must Not Miss – Not exactly a travel guide, but a book that leads you to 111 unusual, hidden spots in the area and tells the often fascinating stories behind them. For people who have already seen the more "touristy" places

20–30 kg/44–66 lb. Two experienced pickers can harvest a maximum of 100 kg/ 220.5 lb olives in a day which makes about 15–18 l/26–32 pt oil. It's not surprising that a litre (about 2 pints) of high quality olive oil easily costs 25 or 30 euros.

HISTORY ON THE LAKE BED

Divers' hearts beat faster: in 2017, a new relic of seafaring history was discovered in Lake Garda. The wreck of a transport ship is located about 150 m/492 ft deep and half-way between Maderno on the

tos on Facebook by visiting "La storia sommersa – Lago di Garda".

HIS MAJESTY THE CODFISH

It's normal for architectural monuments, or famous people, animals and plants to feature on postage stamps. But food?! In Italy, for the first time in the history of philately, this honour has been granted to a recipe for the codfish, the *bacalà alla vicentina* from the area to the south-east of Lake Garda. Since 2017, a terracotta pot with the codfish speciality from Vicenza, a few pieces of codfish and a bowl of

Hard work: ask an olive-grower why 5 euros won't buy a litre (2 pints) of oil

western shore and Torri del Benaco on the east. The accident must have happened during the 17th century. Those who are interested can look at the pho-

polenta are pictured on the 95-cent stamp. Visit *baccala allavicentina.it* to read (in Italian) about how the Norwegian codfish became a classic dish in Vicenza.

FOOD & DRINK

Food in the Lake Garda region, as in the rest of Italy, is more than just nourishment: food is culture. As the lake borders the three regions of Trentino, Lombardy and Veneto, there is no Lake Garda cuisine per se. But, the sheer variety of different regional specialities found in kitchens around the lake makes for an intriguing culinary excursion.

Any holiday on Lake Garda has to include a *lakeside dinner*. Regardless of whether you are on the eastern or western side of the lake, you can choose among a large selection of good *(fish)* restaurants. The culinary common denominator for all three regions is the fact that they draw on Alpine traditions as well as their proximity to the water. The gastronomic palette along the lake includes superb wines, award-winning olive oil, meat from high up in the Alps and, of course, excellent freshwater fish such as trout *(trota)*, Lake Garda carpione *(carpione del Garda)*, Lake Garda whitefish *(coregone)*, vendace *(lavarello)*, pike *(luccio)* and perch *(persico)*.

If you discover *sardine di lago* on the menu you shouldn't miss this opportunity. This is really something quite rare – after all, sardines are normally found in the sea. But there is one subspecies of the herring family that lives in Lake Garda, called the twaite shad in English. These sardines only swim upstream in fresh water to spawn, just like salmon, but somewhere along the

Mushrooms and polenta, whitefish and trout: red wines are served with dishes from the Alps and white wines with fish from the lake

line they seem to have decided to stay in the lake. The sardines are cut into small pieces and mixed with pasta. Spaghetti *con sardine di lago* is still a much-loved delicacy today.

The cuisine in northern Trentino is quite substantial. You will often come across *hearty dishes* such as polenta with rabbit *(coniglio)*, *strangolapreti* (spinach gnocchi, delicious with butter and sage) or *canederli* (dumplings) on the menu. Some of these dishes are almost too heavy for a summer evening

on the lake. They are just a reminder that maybe one should try visiting Lake Garda in winter some time. Everything is quieter then, and if you're shivering outside in a cold wind, hot filling food is just the thing. Another benefit of a winter stay is that December is the *truffle (tartufo)* picking season on the slopes of Monte Baldo. Truffles are a natural delicacy. You should definitely try *carne salada*, which is a kind of cured meat that is truly a *Trentino speciality*. It is either served raw like carpaccio

LOCAL SPECIALITIES

alborelle – fried lake fish

birra alla spina – draught beer; especially with pizza, the Italians don't drink wine very often, but rather beer

bollito misto – stew with boiled chicken, veal and beef, served with pickled sauce, depending on the region

chiaretto – light and fruity rosé wine

cotoletta alla milanese – you might already know these Milan-style breaded cutlets under the name "Wiener Schnitzel"

fiori di zucca ripieni – stuffed courgette flowers (usually filled with ricotta)

giardiniera – the Italian version of mixed pickles

gnocchi – small potato dumplings (photo left)

luccio in salsa – pike in sauce made from fried sardines, a speciality from southern Lake Garda

macedonia – fresh fruit salad

petto di faraona – guinea fowl breast (photo right)

torta sbrisolona – a kind of streusel cake that is broken into pieces, not sliced; perfect with coffee

tortelli di zucca – ravioli stuffed with pumpkin

trota in saor – trout marinated with onions and white wine

as a starter or stewed with beans. Tagliatelle with mushrooms or risotto ai funghi porcini also bring an *Alpine flair* to the table. In this region, *polenta* is very much an indispensable, satisfying side dish.

On the eastern side of the lake bordering Veneto, polenta is also a popular food. But, it is usually finer in texture and creamy because it is made of husked kernels from a lighter coloured corn. Although trade has always flourished in Veneto, and its people have become familiar with foods from Asia and Africa, the local cuisine is still simple and largely influenced by the north. Beans, fish and innards often come into play. As sprawling rice fields can be found to the south of Verona in the Po valley, there are *all sorts of risotti* on menus. When it comes to pasta, the locals prefer thick spaghetti called bigoli. Although the hand-made *Tortellini di Valeggio* from the town of the same name south of Peschiera are no longer an insider's tip, they are still unbelievably delicious.

Lombardy has the largest stretch of the

shoreline, running from Limone in the north on the western shore past Salò and further south to Sirmione. The locals in this area love hearty soups, *savoury stewed meat* or a *spiedo* (skewer) of different kinds of meats with bacon in between that is grilled over an open fire. Of course, you will also find plenty of polenta in Lombardy, too! If you taste buds are yearning for something more adventurous, look for *horse meat*, frog legs or snails on the menu. The lakeside region in Lombardy has the best trattorias and the most star-rated restaurants.

Not only the cuisine is very diverse around the lake, but also the choice of drinks. The hearty food of the north calls for *full-blooded wines*: two delicious red wines exclusively pressed in Trentino are Teroldego and Marzemino. The north is also famous for its grappas. This fragrant, grape-based *pomace liquor* is normally drunk "neat", sometimes flavoured with pine needles, rowan berries or gentian root. The excellent *vino santo* from the area around Lake Toblino is less well known, made from nosiola grapes dried on wooden slats.

On the east shore, the typical wine is red Bardolino. Once discredited as a "mass wine", it is now of good quality. If you want to learn more about it, drive down the *Strada del Vino*. Fine white wines such as the Lugana in particular are found in the south east. As an aperitif or an after-meal drink, keep an eye out for the *sparkling wines* from Franciacorta in the south west, made using the méthode champenoise.

No matter what price bracket you are interested in, around the lake you will find everything from fast-food *take-away pizza* to gourmet-food temples (especially around Salò and Gargna-

no). During peak season and mainly at expensive restaurants you are recommended to *make a reservation*! Connoisseurs who want to enjoy an excursion to Trento should visit the former residence *Palazzo Roccabruna (Thu–Sat 5pm–10pm | www.palazzo roccabruna.it)*. Here, the *Enoteca Provinciale* regularly hosts INSIDER TIP workshops and tastings of local wines and other specialities.

One last tip: the supermarkets and *delicatessen shops* are well-stocked with regional specialities at reasonable prices. There are always local salami and cheeses as well as fresh bread – and tomatoes, mozzarella and basil for a caprese salad. Then head for one of the beaches, a jetty or a slope overlooking the lake and enjoy a *picnic* – buon appetito!

When it comes to wine, Bardolino reigns supreme on the eastern shore

SHOPPING

Taking tasteful souvenirs back home from your stay in Bella Italia is a way of prolonging the enjoyment. No problem: Almost every town round the lake has a weekly market. Whether it's smart shoes you are looking for or top-quality Parmesan, chic handbags or stylish espresso machines, you'll find them here.

Opening times of shops are generally quite flexible as one would tend to expect in Italy. A rule of thumb is 9am until 12pm and 3.30pm until 7pm. In summer, shops are often open till 10pm in many places, or sometimes even later. And in the busiest tourist resorts visitors can even part with their cash on Sundays.

FASHION

Leather goods are still reasonably priced in Italy, especially at markets. Italian designer fashion is available in the brand boutiques of Salò and Peschiera, Desenzano, Riva and Bardolino. A stroll through Sirmione is almost like a visit to a shopping mall: the lanes in the Old Town are full of expensive shops waiting for tourists to come through the door flapping their credit cards.

Meantime, you can often find bargains if you're there in late summer. In end-of-season sales *(saldi)*, many shops discount the goods by 50 percent. The saving is particularly worthwhile with genuine designer clothes.

FOOD & DRINK

Local delicacies make particularly suitable presents, such as the wonderfully mild olive oil from Lake Garda. The best (and cheapest) place to buy it is at a cooperative, for example in Riva, Gargnano or Limone. There are also very good olive-based products at the Olive Museum in Cisano near Bardolino. Alternatives are high-quality or unusual kinds of pasta, wine and grappa, though the latter two are best bought in supermarkets or specialist wine retailers rather than souvenir shops. The packaging may be pretty and appealing to tourists, but the contents are not necessarily the best.

OUTLETS

Outlet shopping is becoming more popular, especially in the south of the lake. Bargain deals on brand-named

Pasta, shoes, sports gear: the weekly markets attract both locals and tourists alike

goods are on offer, for example, directly at Bialetti, a speciality manufacturer of coffee and kitchen equipment. The factory outlet is located in *Coccaglio*, 25 km/15.5 mi west of Brescia *(Via Fogliano 1)*, and offers Bialetti products at a ten to twenty percent discount.

Underwear, hosiery and bikinis are for sale in Avio (Ala-Avio exit from the A 22) at the *Calzedonia Intimissimi Outlet (Via del Lavoro 30/at the corner of Via dei Carri)*.

SHOPPING CENTRES

In addition to the many speciality shops and boutiques, there are also a number of shopping centres in the Lake Garda region, most of which are open seven days a week. These shopping malls are not only a good alternative for rainy days but also if you need to cool down on hot days because they are air-conditioned. With fifty shops, the *Millenium Center (Mon 2pm–8pm, Tue–Sun 9am–8pm | Via del Garda 175)* in Rovereto is the largest shopping centre in Trentino. In Affi, two large shopping centres are situated next to the motorway, *Affi Uno (Mon–Sat 9am–7.30pm | Via Pascoli)* and *Grand'Affi (daily 9am–9pm | located in Canove 1)*.

SPORTS GEAR

With so many sporting types in the Lake Garda area, there is no shortage of suitable sports shops. In Torbole, windsurfers can buy everything they need for their sport, from flashy boards and state-of-the-art equipment to waterproof clothing.

Climbers and mountaineers are catered for (among other places) in Arco, where you can sometimes get cheap mountain gear, while mountain bikers can get spare parts especially in Torbole or Arco.

NORTH SHORE

You can skip that trip to a distant fjord in Norway – go to the north end of Lake Garda instead, which has the same spectacular feel. **The huge sheer mountain faces leave little room for settlements.**

Riva del Garda is the only place with room for growth, since it is situated on the former alluvial plain of the river Sarca. The neighbouring village of Torbole is hemmed in between Monte Brione, the lake shore and the bluff on which the ruins of Penede castle are perched. This situation is what visitors value about Torbole – it creates a wind channel through which the *ora*, *pelér* and *balì* winds regularly blow, much to the enjoyment of the surfing community.

Further south you come to the pretty little village of Malcesine which is, however, often overcrowded. Keen climbers ascend the almost 2000 m-/6562 ft-high peak of Monte Baldo towering over the lake. Directly opposite is Limone, which sometimes seems to groan under the throng of day trippers. The charm of the little place is best savoured early in the morning.

LIMONE SUL GARDA

(138 B5) (* catetq H–J3*) **Even if the pretty village on the north shore is not named after the lemons, the fruits are a trademark of Limone.**

The saying "when life gives you lemons,

A paradise for surfers and mountain bikers: don't miss out on the sporty north shore with its spectacular scenery

make lemonade" has been well known to the residents of Limone for several centuries. When some monks in the Middle Ages brought the exotic fruits to Lake Garda, the Limonesi offered them the best cultivation conditions in their remote fishing village. In 1750, the first fruits could be harvested, but these were not intended for the locals. Instead, they served as precious goods for bartering and they quickly became coveted merchandise. Even in Austria, Russia and England people were keen to obtain North Italian lemons.

Lake Garda still has a guarantee of a perfectly balanced micro-climate, and there is scarcely any concern about freezing temperatures. Nevertheless, the peak tourist season is restricted to the summer months. From November, Limone quietens down for the winter. Many shops, restaurants and hotels close and the parking meters are wrapped in nylon, while the barriers are removed from the multi-storey car park. Now the village is solely for the enjoyment of its approximately 1000 residents.

Limone looks nicest from the water – so do come by boat!

However, they focus more on tourism than on lemon cultivation. Why? In 1861, when the western shore of Lake Garda was part of the newly formed Italy, border and customs controls became obsolete. Lemons from Sicily could then be bought in northern Italy more cheaply than local ones. It was only in the late 20th century when Lake Garda lemons had long since lost their market value that the locals rediscovered their love of the yellow fruits. Today, lemons are used in many dishes and cakes or are sliced thinly and eaten with brown sugar or drunk chilled as Limoncello. Lemons are also a decorative emblem on T-shirts, bags and towels. The name Limone has nothing to do with the fruit and is derived from the Latin *limes* = a border, as for many years this was the frontier between Austria and Italy: so what ...

SIGHTSEEING

LIMONAIA DEL CASTEL
Smell the fine scent of citrus trees in this renovated 18th-century conservatory. Today, the *limonaia* is also an open-air museum whose gardens are sometimes open until midnight in summer. *April–Oct daily 10am–10pm, Nov–March irregular opening hours (tel. 03 65 95 40 08) | clearly signposted*

MUSEO DEL TURISMO
The local community has taken great care to collect old photos, newspaper articles and much more about the (tourism) history of the village. The small museum is in the centre of the Old Town and opens until late. Admission is free. What more do you want? *March–Oct daily 10am–10pm | Via Monsignor Daniele Comboni 3*

PARCO VILLA BOGHI

Had enough of the crowds in the narrow lanes of the Old Town? Then relax in the manicured gardens of Villa Boghi. Here, there is also a small fishing museum and an old-fashioned *limonaia*, a conservatory for cultivating lemons.

FOOD & DRINK

INSIDER TIP ▶ DALCO

Enjoy Mediterranean fish specialities or rustic alpine cuisine high above the sea on the sprawling terrace or in the garden with a pool. A view of Monte Baldo at sunset is also included at this very trendy restaurant with a bit of a lounge flair and delicious food! Daily | *Via Prealzo 4a | tel. 03 65 95 46 35| Budget–Expensive*

HOTEL AL RIO SE'

Regulars have been returning to this small hotel somewhat off the beaten track for decades. It's very quiet on the terrace of the restaurant where you can enjoy a wonderful fillet of trout with fresh sage and butter. *Open daily April–Oct | Via Nova 12 | tel. 03 65 95 41 82 | www.hotelalriose.com | Budget*

SHOPPING

COOPERATIVA AGRICOLA
POSSIDENTI OLIVETI ☻

The shop of this cooperative of "olive-grove owners" does not only sell olio d'oliva extra vergine but other related products, such as olives and paste. All olives are grown locally. *Via Campaldo 10 and Via IV Novembre 29 | www.oleificio limonesulgarda.it*

FRUTTO DEL GARDA ☻

Are you a fan of citrus fruits? Then visit this small organic farm (please phone beforehand!). The Risatti couple have lovingly planted (by hand) about 150 plants and use the fruits to make jams, liqueurs and syrups. Everything is organic! *Via Campaldo 12 | tel. 34 01 08 50 19 | www.fruttodelgarda.it*

MARKET

From April to October, there is a market in the town centre every Tuesday.

LEISURE, SPORTS & BEACHES

There is a tiny pebbly beach at the north end of the promenade in the Old Town, and the Spiaggia del Tifù with beach volleyball on the southern fringe. South of the large carpark you will find the large public pebbly beach. *Surfing Lino (Spiaggia Foce Fiume San Giovanni | tel. 33 84 09 74 90 | www.surfinglino.com)*

★ **Museo Castello Scaligero in Malcesine**
Natural history with a touch of literary genius in Malcesine's Scaliger Castle → p. 36

★ **Funivia Malcesine – Monte Baldo**
Far-reaching views from the cable car with panoramic windows and from the summit → p. 40

★ **Castello di Arco**
Walk through the olive groves up to the castle high above the town → p. 48

★ **Riva del Garda**
For over 100 years writers and other visitors have been seduced by the charm of the mainly traffic-free town on the north shore → p. 41

MARCO POLO HIGHLIGHTS

offers cat sailing and wind surfing lessons. From May to October, the local tourist association organises guided walks and hikes. The tours are free and there is a route for everyone, ranging from a demanding hike to the Bonaventura Segala lodge, a walk along the "sunny path" or excursions to olive groves. For more information, visit the tourist information centre or *www.visitlimonesulgarda.com*.

ENTERTAINMENT

Night life is not the main priority in Limone. After dinner, you can stroll through the streets of the old town centre. You'll have no trouble finding someplace to drink a spritzer. In summer, there are also concerts.

WHERE TO STAY

GARDA

A camping site with a private beach. *Via IV Novembre 10 | located in Fasse sul Lago | tel. 03 65 95 45 50*

LE PALME

If living right in the centre is what you want, this is the place. Le Palme occupies a 17th-century villa. Minimum stay 3 nights. *30 rooms | Via Porto 36 | tel. 03 65 95 46 81| www.sunhotels.it | Moderate–Expensive*

RESIDENCE RONCHI

This little complex of holiday flats with a communal pool is situated above the village in the olive groves. Lovely views over the lake. Just 500 m/1640 ft from the centre. *8 flats | Via Milanesa 3a | tel. 03 65 95 46 96 | www.appartamentiron chi.com | Moderate*

HOTEL SOLE

Right plum in the middle of the village, directly on the lakeside and just a hop, skip and jump from where the boats come in – and with a view like in an oil painting. Make sure you ask for a room with a view of the lake! *38 rooms | Via Guglielmo Marconi 36 | tel. 03 65 95 40 55 | www.hotel solelimone.com | Budget–Moderate*

INFORMATION

Via IV Novembre 29 | tel. 03 65 95 47 20 | www.visitlimonesulgarda.com, www.gar dalombardia.com

MALCESINE

(138 B5–6) (*Ш J4*) Although Malcesine with its population of about 3700 is one of the most popular holiday destinations on the lake, in the picturesque centre it retains its pleasant and relaxing atmosphere.

The ● Scaliger Castle sits majestically above the medieval centre. Small squares, arcades and narrow alleys are everywhere and almost all lead to the old harbour. But if you only stroll along the shore, you miss some of the atmosphere of the place. Don't forget to visit the castle on any account – the wonderful views make this more than worthwhile.

SIGHTSEEING

MUSEO CASTELLO SCALIGERO ★

The museum in the castle has been carefully modernised at great expense. The Goethe Room has copies of his drawings of Lake Garda. Goethe unpacked his paints and brushes inside the castle and nearly got arrested as a result: He was taken for a Habsburg spy who was not only interested in the castle's appearance but also in its use as a military stronghold. When he told the guards he was from Frankfurt, everything turned out well. *April–Oct daily 9.30am–6pm, Nov–March varying opening times*

PALAZZO DEI CAPITANI DEL LAGO

The palace by the port was built by the Scaligers in the 13th century – the un-

RE LEAR

One of the classier places to eat in Malcesine. You sit under a vaulted ceiling without it being at all rustic; very cosy overlooking the little square to the front. The gourmet table d'hôte costs 45 euros and is money well spent. *Closed Tue | Piazza Cavour 23 | tel. 04 57 40 06 16 | Expensive*

Which is the most beautiful castle on the lake? Malcesine's Rocca Scaligera ranks highly on the list

mistakable design of the battlements was borrowed from the Venetians. Nowadays it serves as the Town Hall, where exhibitions are put on from time to time. You should then visit the small palm garden directly on the lake.

FOOD & DRINK

CA' DEL TOCIO

In this small idyllic restaurant high above the lake, Mamma Angiolina prepares regional dishes such as gnocchi according to old recipes in her kitchen. *Daily April–Nov | Via San Michele 31 | tel. 34 42 67 76 74 | Budget*

INSIDER TIP SPECKSTUBE

The traditional-style Speckstube with its self-service beer garden is down-to-earth and family-friendly. It is also very popular among the locals, offering a change from all the many typical Italian restaurants. Kids can run about the playground. *Daily March–Oct | Via Navene Vecchia 139 | tel. 04 57 40 11 77 | www.speckstube.com | Budget*

SHOPPING

INSIDER TIP CONSORZIO OLIVICOLTORI

550 smallholders from Malcesine send

their olives here for processing. The shop also stocks other local products. *Via Navene 21 | www.oliomalcesine.it*

MARKET
Every Saturday morning in the square by the Municipio.

LEISURE, SPORTS & BEACHES

A safe footpath and cycle path leads to Navene, 5 km/3.1 mi to the north, so the beaches are easy to reach. There is a tiny bathing area beneath the castle, plus a sunbathing area south of the promenade.
The business renting mountain bikes (from 25 euros a day) also has flats to rent in the same building at the bottom of the cable car: *Xtreme (Via Navene Vecchia 10 | tel. 04 57 40 01 05 | www.xtreme malcesine.com)*.

LOW BUDGET

A tourist bus operates within the parish of Malcesine, from Navene to Cassone, running daily from 8am–3pm and 4pm–1am back and forth. The journey costs just 1 euro. To be recommended especially on market days.

A number of jazz events under the heading *Gardajazz (www.garda jazz.com)* are held in June and July in towns and villages on Lake Garda that are in the district of Trentino. Apart from concerts in the Rocca in Riva and in Arco castle, for example, there are also several ● jazz cafés. Entrance to all events is free!

Paragliders take off from below the top station, more info available from *Paragliding Malcesine (Via Gardesana 228 | tel. 33 56 11 29 02 | www.paragliding malcesine.it)*. Tandem flights can be booked with the flight school *Fly 2 Fun (tel. 33 49 46 97 57 | www.tandempara gliding.eu)*.

ENTERTAINMENT

Malcesine's Old Town is bursting with life in summer until midnight.

ART CAFÉ
If you want a change from wine and the usual alcoholic drinks, have a milk shake in the smart Art Café instead. Piazza Turazza 12

OSTERIA SANTO CIELO
A small osteria where you can get light dishes, for example bruschette or a cheese platter, but the extensive wine list is more notable. The Dutch owner, Hella, came to Italy because she fell in love and stayed on because of the cuisine. *Piazza Turazza 11 | tel. 34 87 45 13 45| www.osteriasantocielo.com*

PUB VAGABONDO
Here, cyclists and kite-surfers swap banter about wind and wild rides until 3am. Lots of locals, too. *Via Porta Orientale 1*

WHERE TO STAY

On the lakeside road in the direction of Navene there is one campsite after another.

HOTEL DU LAC
The rooms of this elegant hotel have huge a panoramic windows facing the lake. The hotel is directly on the promenade, modern in design and impeccable

The glorious north shore: the impressive backdrop of the lake and mountains

in style. *37 rooms | Via Gardesana 63 | tel. 04 57 40 01 56 | www.dulac.it | Expensive*

AMBIENTHOTEL PRIMA LUNA

Modern, elegant, friendly and welcoming – the hotel is a must for fans of design and architecture. The breakfast is extremely generous. *38 rooms | Via Gardesana 165 | tel. 04 57 40 03 01 | www.primalunahotel.com | Moderate–Expensive*

VILLA ALBA

Some of the rooms have splendid views of the lake. The owner is a motorbike fan. There's space for the bikes in the garage, a high-pressure cleaner and tools – and an extensive breakfast buffet. *12 rooms | Via Gardesana 196 | tel. 04 57 40 02 77 | www.hotelvillaalba.it | Budget–Moderate*

Via Gardesana 238 | tel. 57 40 00 44 | www.malcesinepiu.it

WHERE TO GO

BRENZONE AND CASSONE
(138 B6, 142–143 C–D1) (*Ⓜ H–J 4–5*)

If you head south along the lake, it's not far to *Cassone* and then to *Brenzone* which is really a collection of villages between Malcesine and Torri del Benaco. The source of the Aril River is in picturesque Cassone. The river is only about 175 m/574 ft and flows into the lake. In the small harbour there is the carefully renovated fishermen's museum ● *Museo del Lago (Tue–Sun, in winter only Sun 10am–12 noon and 3pm–6pm).*

The many small, original villages of Brenzone are scattered at the foot of Monte Baldo. Bikers and walkers especially appreciate this, as many trekking routes and downhill trails lead along the slopes. For example, you can only walk or bike to the picturesque medieval village INSIDER TIP *Campo*, which is high up at 230 m/755 ft and in a remote position in the middle of centuries-old olive groves. Cultural events are often held here

Far-reaching panoramic views: impressive views for day-trippers to Monte Baldo – already on the way via the Funivia cable car

in summer. The hiking paths begin in Marniga and Castelletto.

Stroll also through the narrow streets of ☙ Castello di Brenzone – it's much more peaceful here than down by the lake and the views of the west shore are fantastic. Directly on the beach is the *Belfiore Park Hotel (32 rooms | Via Zanardelli 3 | located in Porto | tel. 04 57 42 01 02 | www. consolinihotels.it | Expensive)*. Kitesurfers stay at the boutique hotel *Club da Baia (9 rooms | Via 20 Settembre 54 | located in Magugnano | tel. 34 82 61 93 83 | www.clubdabaia.com | Budget–Moderate)* with its own kitesurfing school. Information: *Via Zanardelli 38 | tel. 04 57 42 00 76 | www.brenzone.it*

EREMO SANTI BENIGNO E CARO ☙ (138 B6) (*Ⓜ J4*)

The hermitage of the Blessed Benignus and Carus is in Cassone. It can be reached by a two-hour walk from the middle station of the cable car from Malcesine. The path is signposted and easy to find. The church is only open a few days a year. Processions from Malcesine take place on 12 April, 27 July, 16 August and on the third Sunday in October.

FUNIVIA MALCESINE–MONTE BALDO ★ ☙ (138 B–C5) (*Ⓜ J4*)

The Monte Baldo cable car climbs 1700 m/5577 ft from Malcesine via the middle station of San Michele to the summit. That's a double treat since you get a lot of time to look at the view as well as a ride. The cabins are glazed all round and turn on their own axis. As this is a very popular excursion, on some days expect long queues! The only way to avoid the crowds is to get up early and catch one of the earliest cable cars before the crowds arrive. Mountain bikes may also be taken, but only at specified times. Once at the top, walkers and mountain-bikers have panoramic ● ☙ paths in all degrees of difficulty to choose from. From June to October, a variety of events are organised, ranging from culinary walks with tastings to jazz & blues concerts to photo exhibitions (information and tickets are available on the cable car's website). A particular treat is the hike on the ⛷ *Monte Altissimo* and to INSIDER TIP *Rifugio Altissimo Damiano Chiesa (tel. 04 64 86 71 30 | www.rifugioaltissimo. it)*, which takes a few hours. The view from the peak is a fitting reward for the effort, and lodge-keeper Danny Zampiccoli serves up local specialities (*Budget*). If you would like, you can stay the night in the Rifugio and enjoy the star-studded night sky. The ⛷ *Baita dei Forti (daily | tel. 04 57 40 03 19 | www.baitadei forti.com | Budget–Moderate)* is near the summit of the cable car. Dishes include the *Trittico Baldo* – a spicy trio of venison goulash, mushroom ragout and polenta. You can also stay the night in one of the six rooms (*Budget–Moderate*). In the evenings, you have the mountain almost to yourself, and the view of the lake with the lights on the shores is unforgettable. *Daily 8am–5/6/7pm depending on the season | return fare 20, one-way 15, with a mountain bike 20 euros | www. funiviedelbaldo.it*

RIVA DEL GARDA

MAP INSIDE BACK COVER
(138 C3) (𝕄 J2) **The small ★ town with its population of 16,000 feels close to many of those living in central Europe – and not just in geographical terms.**

Many people feel quite at home as they approach Lake Garda via the Brenner Pass. It's not surprising: the northern shore is popular with German visitors and particularly the picturesque town of Riva nestling between the lake, rocky mountains and olive trees. But despite the numerous tourists, the second biggest town on the lake retains its special charm.

Enjoy this wonderful mixture of Italian *dolce vita* and Alpine nature-lover's paradise!

How did this evolve? In the 19th century when the town was still governed by Austria-Hungary, Riva was already popular and became a busy spa town. First, it was only visited by the Habsburgs, and later American millionaires arrived as well as Russian aristocrats. They were attracted by the mild climate, culture and numerous places for excursions. Not much has changed until today. The town and its lively pedestrian zone, many shops and narrow alleys is a popular resort all year round – for families as well as holiday-makers with an interest in all kinds of sports. The surrounding mountains satisfy the demands of bikers and climbers. Surfers and sailors enjoy the constant winds and water sports fans practice their art along extensive bathing beaches. At sunset on the piazza, you can enjoy an Italian *aperitivo* and a large *gelato* after dinner.

SIGHTSEEING

FORTRESS AND MUSEUM

What was once designed to instil fear, now looks rather romantic. In the 12th century there was a moated castle here, and now colourful fishing boats float on the water and scare away the ducks. Inside the castle is the *Museo Alto Garda MAG (mid-March–May and Oct Tue–Sun, June–Sept daily 10am–6pm | www.mu seoaltogarda.it)* with an art gallery and exhibition about the town's history. During the Advent season, Father Christmas even visits here.

The Alps soar majestically above, while palm trees grow below: the charm of Riva

CHIESA DELL'INVIOLATA

The striking octagonal church was built outside the Old Town in the 17th century. It is considered the finest Baroque church in Trentino.

TORRE APPONALE

The town's 34 m-/111.5 ft-high landmark that makes pictures of Riva so unmistakable, was built in the 13th century to protect the harbour. The busy Piazza III Novembre, the heart of the Old Town, spreads out at the foot of the tower.

FOOD & DRINK

LA FATTORIA

This restaurant somewhat outside the town centre behind the fairgrounds offers lots of space for families or large groups. The pizzas and the friendly service are also fantastic, drawing many locals especially at weekends. *Daily | Via Marone 9 | tel. 04 64 55 78 44 | Moderate*

LA MONTANARA

The chequered tablecloths go with the rustic cuisine, such as Trentino horse steaks or penne with taleggio cheese. *Closed Wed | Via Montanara 20 | tel. 04 64 55 48 57 | Budget–Moderate*

NUOVO 900 DA LUCIO

Whether you're in the mood for an aperitif, a glass of wine after dinner, or a proper meal, the Nuovo 900 da Lucio is the place to go. It is a rustic-chic wine bar as well as a restaurant with home-style cooking. The dishes are simple, the selection is small, but the quality is excellent. Live music on Thursdays. *Closed Wed | Via Gazzoletti 8 | tel. 04 64 56 76 29 | Budget–Moderate*

PIZZOTECA

Authentic pizza dough, thin and crispy and with fresh ingredients – the locals in Riva love this and enjoy dining here. **INSIDER TIP** Pizza Brisa with ceps, buffalo Mozzarella and rocket is delicious! The garden is pleasant in summer. *In winter, closed Tue | Viale Baruffaldi 1 | tel. 04 64 52 04 00 | Budget*

AL VOLT

For an authentic and idyllic dinner experience in the midst of so many touristy restaurants, head to Al Volt in an old palazzo in the centre of Riva. The fish and carpaccio are a delight, not to mention the good wines and friendly service as well as the lovingly decorated interior with red tablecloths. *Closed Mon | Via Fiume 73 | tel. 04 64 55 25 70 | www.ris torantealvolt.com | Moderate–Expensive*

SHOPPING

AGRARIA

An oil mill for local olive-growers, wine cellar and rural store for local specialities. You can join a guided tour and/or buy typical gourmet delicacies from this region. *District San Nazzaro 4 | store.agririva.it*

ALIMENTARI MORGHEN ◔

Pasta and rice, vegetables, coffee, olives – this shop has everything you'd expect of an Italian grocer – except that INSIDER TIP everything here is organic. And for those who like dark bread, there's wholemeal as well. *Viale Rovereto 101*

ERRELUCE

All the smart designer lamps that cost a bomb back home are not exactly cheap here either, but this small shop also has goods at reduced prices. *Viale dei Tigli 21c*

MARKET

In summer, the market is held every second and fourth Wed of the month in *Viale Dante.*

LEISURE, SPORTS & BEACHES

Riva has one of the largest and best public beaches on the whole lake. The popular *Spiaggia Sabbioni* is a pretty pebble beach with trees, a bar and artificial bathing islands. You will find one beach after the other along the shoreline to Torbole. There are several places to rent bikes for those without their own; specialist outlets also have mountain bikes for the more sporty as well as conventional bikes. Surf-

ing and sailing schools are dotted along the beach. If you are looking for a bit of relaxation and pampering while on holiday, book an open-air yoga session or Thai massage with Marco Mantegazza from *Fior di Loto (Via Marconi 17 | tel. 4 64 51 92 84 | www.fiordilotothai.com) in Arco.*

ENTERTAINMENT

PUB ALL'OCA

Riva's oldest pub is the hangout of the locals. *Daily | Via Santa Maria 15 | www. puballoca.it*

RIVA BAR

The cocktails and ● *aperitivi* are legendary with their amazing choice of snacks from vegetable sticks to mini-pizzas. During the day, coffee is the beverage of choice at Riva Bar. *Daily | Largo Medaglie d'Oro 1 | www.rivabar.it*

SAILING BAR

The best place for a traditional Italian Aperol Spritz and cool music. The view from the ☆ rooftop terrace is fantastic! *Viale Rovereto 136*

WHERE TO STAY

ACETAIA DEL BALSAMICO TRENTINO ☆

The architecture of this modern *agriturismo* takes a bit of getting used to. Nonetheless, it is a wonderful place to taste the fine balsamic vinegar as well as typical local products such as wine and cheese. The Acetaia is situated outside Riva with a superb view of Lake Garda. *7 rooms, 3 suites | Strada di San Zeno 2 | Cologna di Tenno | tel. 04 64 55 00 64 | www. acetaiadelbalsa mico.it | Moderate*

HOTEL ANTICO BORGO

Ideal for fans of the Old Town: shops, bars and the hubbub of tourists are on the doorstep. But it's still fairly peaceful. Fabulous 🌿 rootop terrace! *61 rooms | Via Diaz 15 | tel. 04 64 55 43 67 | www. anticoborgogarda.it | Moderate*

LIDO PALACE

When this hotel first opened in 1899, it was popular among the upper aristocracy. Although it later fell into disrepair, it has been completely renovated with its own park located directly on the lake shore, which now reigns over the local hotel scene. *28 rooms | Viale Carducci 10 | tel. 04 64 02 18 99 | www. lido-palace.it | Expensive*

OSTELLO BENACUS

Three-storey youth hostel with two twin rooms and two rooms with four beds, each with their own bathroom, as well as dormitories with lockers. *Piazza Cavour 14 | tel. 04 64 55 49 11 | www.ostel loriva.com | Budget*

VILLA MARIA

This small guest house within walking distance of the Old Town is quiet if you take a room at the back. The rooms are modestly furnished, but the service makes up for that. Breakfast with fruit and cakes. *10 rooms | Viale dei Tigli 19 | tel. 04 64 55 22 88 | www.garnimaria.com | Budget*

INFORMATION

Largo Medaglie d'Oro al Valor Militare 5 | tel. 04 64 55 44 44 | www.gardatrentino.it

WHERE TO GO

CASCATA DEL VARONE ●
(138 B3) (*ⓜ J2*)

What peacefully shimmers up in Lago di Tenno drops 100 m/328 ft here into the valley below with a roar. The walk is rel-

atively short, but still quite impressive, loud and wet. Don't forget rain gear! *March and Oct daily 9am–5pm, April and Sept 9am–6pm, May–Aug 9am–7pm, Nov–Feb Sun 10am–5pm | www.cascata-varone.com*

LAGO DI LEDRO (138 A–B3) (*ⓜ H2*)

If it gets too hot or too crowded for you down on Lake Garda, you can take a shortish trip (about 10 km/6.2 mi, and also easy by bus!) into the mountains. On the high plain of Ledro Valley *(www. valledilledro.com)* and on Lake Ledro, which is ideal for swimming, it is not only a few degrees cooler but there is also the *Museo delle Palafitte* (see p. 119) in Molina di Ledro. At the far end of the valley and near a lovely beach is the *Hotel Garni Minigolf (12 rooms | Viale Foletto 3 | Pieve di Ledro | tel. 04 64 59 21 37 | www.garni minigolf.it | Budget)*. At the classy, rustic *Baita Santa Lucia (closed Mon | Via Santa Lucia 36 | Bezzecca | tel. 04 64 59 12 90 | www.valledilledro.com/baita | Moderate)*, you should try the typical Trentino specialities such as barley soup or homemade pasta.

TENNO AND LAGO DI TENNO
(138 B–C 2–3) (*ⓜ J2*)

A winding road leads 6 km/3.7 mi uphill to Tenno. As you arrive in the village, it's worth visting the Frizzi family who run the *Ristorante Castello (closed Wed | Via Castello 3 | tel. 04 64 50 06 38 | Budget)*, run by the Frizzi family, is worth a visit – they have INSIDER TIP very good *carne salada*. From Tenno, you can take a delightful walk along the *Sentiero del Salt* to the INSIDER TIP *Canale di Tenno*, a well looked-after medieval village.

Go a few miles further and you come to *Lago di Tenno*, a green mountain lake with a small beach. If you would like to enjoy the untouched nature around Lake

Tenno in peace, book one of the six family-run apartments at Al Trovante *(located in Lago di Tenno 6 | tel. 04 64 50 21 55 | www.altrovante.com | Moderate)*.

TORBOLE

(138 C3–4) (⌁ J2) **Torbole (stressed on the first 'o') has a population of 900 and is where the youthful, keen sporty types meet to take advantage of the winds. These are constant and provide ideal conditions that surfers particularly appreciate.**

Where there were previously only several colourful fishing cottages, which were positioned in an idyllic spot between the lake and mountains, today hotels of all price groups are situated between the olive trees. The centre of the Old Town is small and easy to find one's way around.

Mountain bikers and particularly surfers seem to love Torbole, and this is reflected in the nightlife. If there is a party town on the north shore of Lake Garda, then this is it.

SIGHTSEEING

CASA DEL DAZIO

The light yellow, narrow 18th-century building in the small harbour is regarded by many as the emblem of Torbole. It is a former customs house: until the end of the First World War, this was the frontier between Austria and Italy.

SANT'ANDREA ☆

The uphill path is narrow and steep, but it is worth the effort because of the beautiful view over the lake. The 12th century church used to be simple and was remodelled in the Baroque period. Presumably

Mediterranean atmosphere, alpine surroundings: Torbole, a windsurfers' Mecca

some of the locals sat as models for the realistic altar painting.

FOOD & DRINK

RISTORANTE BENACO ☼

Even if the magnificent lakeside position makes you suspect that this is a tourist trap, there is no need to worry. This traditional restaurant has Mediterranean flair. Inside the hotel is a highly recommended INSIDER TIP collection of paintings by artists who stayed here. *Daily | Via Benaco 35 | tel. 04 64 50 53 64 | www.onbenaco.com | Budget–Moderate*

HOTEL CENTRALE

The food here is excellent, whether it's fish or just a pizza. Sitting under a wide awning overlooking the piazza is also very pleasant. *Closed Wed | Piazza Goethe 13 | tel. 04 64 50 52 34 | www.hotelcentraletorbole.it | Moderate*

BAR ALLA SEGA ● ☼

The ultimate panoramic view! Guests who sit down to eat a panino shielded by the glass panel on the terrace can remove their pullovers in March and enjoy the view of the lake and 2000 m/6562 ft high mountains. *March–Oct daily | Via Passseggiata dell'Ora 1*

SURFERS GRILL

Hungry surfers know it already: they besiege this popular restaurant, where – as the name says – grilled dishes are the speciality. *Closed Mon | Via Sarca Vecchio 5 | tel. 04 64 50 59 30 | www.surfersgrill.it | Moderate*

LA TERRAZZA ☼

This classier restaurant is nicest in the evenings. The fish specialities (unfortunately none too cheap) are a good accompaniment to the wonderful sunset (free of charge). *Reserve early. Closed Tue | Via Benaco 24 | tel. 04 64 50 60 83 | www.allaterrazza.com | Expensive*

VILLA CIAN ☼

Its pizza and pasta and the brilliant view of the lake tend to attract a younger public. Lots of partying. *Closed Tue | Via Sarca Vecchio 11 | tel. 04 64 50 52 54 | www.villaciantorbole.it | Moderate*

LEISURE, SPORTS & BEACHES

A long beach of small pebbles stretches from near the town centre to Monte Brione. Bike rental companies are just as well represented in Torbole as surf schools and places to hire boards, such as the *Shaka Surf Center (located in Conca d'Oro | www.shakasurfcenter.com), Vasco Renna Surf (www.vascorenna.com)* in the marina and *Surf-Segnana (Foci del Sarca | www.surfsegnana.it)*.

Healing thermal waters bubble away in spa pools of the *modern Garda Thermae (staggered opening hours and prices | Via Linfano 52 | www.gardathermae.it)*. It has three pools, various saunas, a beauty centre, a medical spa and a fitness room. For families, a trip to the adventure park INSIDER TIP ▶ *Busatte Parco Avventura (www.busatteadventure.it)* surrounded by evergreens high above Torbole, is truly worthwhile. The park has a BMX track, a bike park, a ropes course, a large meadow, a playground and a ● restaurant – ideal for (grand)parents looking to relax and enjoy a cappuccino or birra while watching all the fun. A few steps further, you'll find the start of the a panoramic trail from Busatte to Tempesta. Although this is not a fixed-rope route, clambering up and down metal ladders and steps in the cliff face does demand a head for heights. The return journey can be done by bus.

Ristorante and Hotel Centrale: Pizza and *pesce* at the Piazza

ENTERTAINMENT

After the sun goes down, the nightlife scene goes bar hopping. The first stop is *Aurora Bar (Via Matteotti 55)* with its colourful beanbag chairs and sun sails and then it's on to trendy *Wind's Bar (Via Matteotti 9 | www.windsbar.com)*, but you can always reverse the order. *The Cutty Sark Pub (Via Pontalti 2)* is the real hotspot at weekends.

WHERE TO STAY

CASA BERTOLINI

Flats with one or several rooms are available in three different buildings. Small, modern INSIDERTIP *Casa 3* is particularly attractive, located on the bank of the Sarca in a park. *Via Pasubio 10 | tel. 04 64 50 52 77 | www.casabertolini.com | Moderate*

CAMPING

As windsurfers prefer to shell out for a new board rather than an expensive bed, many of them come in a dormobile or with a tent. For this reason, there are masses of camp sites in Torbole to cater for them, e. g. *Camping Europa (tel. 04 64 50 58 88 | www.campingeuropa torbole.it)*, *Camping Maroadi (tel. 04 64 50 51 75 | www.campingmaroadi. it)* and the more basis sites *Camping al Cor (tel. 04 64 50 52 22 | www.camping-al-cor.com)* and *Camping Al Porto (tel. 04 64 50 58 91 | www.campingalporto.it)*.

AKTIVHOTEL SANTA LUCIA

Sports-lovers will feel at home here, and not just because of the large breakfast buffet. The hotel is situated away from all the hustle and bustle, and it is an ideal starting point for mountain bike tours, hikes or surfing. *36 rooms | Via Santa*

Lucia 6 | tel. 04 64 50 51 40 | www.aktiv hotel.it | Moderate

HOTEL SANTONI

This free-style hotel caters particularly to active holidaymakers. Breakfast is served until 11am and offers in-

For those who like climbing steep walls: Arco's legendary Colodri Wall is a must

clude lots of extras such as free guided tours. *36 rooms | Via Strada Granda 6 | tel. 04 64 50 59 66 | www.hotelsantoni. com | Moderate–Expensive*

VILLA EMMA

This basic, family-run hotel is a good deal for the money. The pizzeria is also popular among the locals. *14 rooms | Via Coize 39 | tel. 04 64 50 57 28 | www.villa emma.com | Budget*

VILLA STELLA

Angelica greets her guests warmly in peaceful surroundings. The garden with a pool is not just relaxing for cyclists. Bikes are available on-site. *44 rooms | Via Strada Granda 104 | tel. 04 64 50 53 54 | www.villastella.it | Moderate*

INFORMATION

Lungolago Conca d'Oro 25 | tel. 04 64 50 51 77 | www.gardatrentino.it

WHERE TO GO

ARCO (138 C3) (*∭ J2*)

Holidaymakers and mountain sports fans who prefer more peaceful surroundings head 6 km/3.7 mi to the small town of Arco (pop. 18,000) with its historic centre that sits below a castle atop a massive cliff. To the north of the castle, the 300 m-/984 ft-high Colodri wall is part of a legendary climbing area with a **INSIDER TIP** via ferrata. Local mountain guide groups and a mountaineering school offer guided tours, canyoning and climbing lessons.

The best place to park is the *Foro Boario* car park right in the centre of town. Stroll through the pedestrian zone and check out the sports shops, pubs and ice cream vendors – the cold treats at *Tarifa* are quite yummy *(Via Giovanni Segantini 51)* and bars. Then walk about 20 minutes through the narrow streets of the old town centre and lovely olive groves up to ★ *Castello di Arco (daily 10am–4pm, April–Sept until 7pm)*. You do not have to pay an entrance fee unless you want to explore past the ⚜ jousting area with its amazing views. On the way back, stop at *Parco Arciducale (April–Sept daily 8am–7pm, Oct–March 9am–4pm | short.travel/gar2)* and watch the turtles sunning themselves on the small pond.

This botanical garden with its trees and shrubs, some of which are exotic, was planted under the aegis of the Habsburg Archduke at the turn of the 20th century. On the way back to the town centre, you will go past a casino, which used to be frequented by the upper aristocracy and where the Empress Sisi once danced. Today, you can sit elegantly on the veranda of the INSIDER TIP *Caffè Casinò (Viale delle Palme 6 | www.caffecasinoarco. it)* and enjoy a cappuccino or a *panino*. Across the street, there is the *Tourist Information Centre (Viale delle Palme 1 | tel. 04 64 53 22 55 | www.gardatrentino.it)*. Climbers tend to meet at *Caffè Conti d'Arco (closed Thu | Piazza Prospero Marchetti 3)* and mountain bikers prefer the *Caffè Trentino (Piazza III Novembre 10 | www.caffetrentino.com)*.

If you enjoy vegetarian food, book (!) a table at the INSIDER TIP vegan restaurant *Veganima (Closed Wed | Viale Magnolie 29 | tel. 04 64 51 97 64 | Budget)*. The vegetable curries and Ricotta cheese cake are delicious.

Sleep in elegant white surroundings at *Garni on the Rock (19 rooms | Vicolo Ere 23 | tel. 04 64 51 68 25 | www.garni ontherock.com | Moderate)* on the castle rock. You can also find your inner peace with the help of seminars offered in the Buddhist centre ● *Kushi Ling (Laghel 19 | www.kushi-ling.com)* located above Arco.

MARMITTE DEI GIGANTI
(138 C3) (*ᗩ J2*)

Whether the Marmitte dei Giganti look like huge cauldrons from which giants quench their thirst – as the name implies – is a matter of conjecture. Whatever you want to believe, these glacial hollows – formed in the ice age – are impressive. Water from melting snow mixed with sand and gravel swirled around at great speed and scooped out these dips in the rock. The sometimes extreme overhanging cliffs are popular among climbers.

MAROCCHE DI DRO (139 D2) (*ᗩ K1*)

This spectacular outcropping of rocks created during the Ice Age is located about 15 km/9.3 mi to the north near the town of Dro. You can trace fossil evidence of dinosaurs on some of the rocks. It is also interesting to look at all the plants that have adapted to this rocky world. A lovely cycle tour leads from Torbole to this biotope.

MONTE BRIONE 🌿 (138 C3) (*ᗩ J2*)

Torbole and Riva are separated by the massive 376 m-/1234 ft-high limestone bluff of Monte Brione. Waymarked trails lead to the top. The most remarkable viewpoint of Lake Garda is from the summit – on top of a bunker built by the Austrians in 1860.

NAGO (138 C3) (*ᗩ J2*)

In Nago, which is a continuation of Torbole, are the 🌿 ruins of *Castello Penede*. It was destroyed by French troops around 1700 due to its strategically important location. The fortress boasted a gunpowder magazine and watchtower as well as a drawbridge. From Nago castle, a 🌿 path with panoramic views leads to the restored ruins of the fortress. A walk along the path alone is worth it for the views.

The more than 100-year-old, traditional 🍃 *Eco Hotel Zanella (33 rooms | Via Sighele 1 | tel. 04 64 50 51 54 | www. ecohotelzanella.com | Budget–Moderate)*, in the centre of the village, has newly established itself as an environmentally-friendly hotel. The breakfast table is piled high with local produce; soaps and shower gel are organic and biodegradable. Small pool in the inner courtyard.

EAST SHORE

If you ask Lake Garda fans which is the "better side" of the lake, this is likely to cause a real dilemma. You will find proponents for each side, but don't worry: the simplest response is that every spot on the lake is glorious! This is because of the impressive panoramic views that surprise and delight visitors.

The east shore of the lake is known as the "olive riviera": the silvery leaves catch the sunlight and stretch as far as the eye can see. For amateurs as well as for serious olive-growers the harvest season is during late autumn. Everybody helps – grown-ups and young children alike; and depending on how ripe they are, the green or black olives are shaken from the trees using sticks and special devices. The fruits are – as ever – collected by hand. And those who have no olive trees are likely to have vines, at least further in the south.

The east shore is easy to explore using the lakeside Gardesana Orientale. The narrow road connects Torbole in the north via Torri del Benaco, which is grouped around the old harbour, and busy Garda with Bardolino, the biggest town on the east shore, and with the small medieval town Lazise. It is a delightful tour, which offers plenty of cultural attractions, several Scaliger castles and wonderful Venetian palazzi. However, you should leave plenty of time for this trip, as during the peak season the Gardesana Orientale is particularly busy with road traffic.

Narrow streets in historic towns and leisure parks: the "Olive Riviera" on the Venetian side could equally well be called the "Wine Riviera"

BARDOLINO

MAP INSIDE BACK COVER
(142 C3) (*∅ H6*) **If someone only knows one place on Lake Garda, then it will probably be Bardolino – the traditional tourist destination.**

And should someone not know Lake Garda at all, then at least this place name may ring a bell: Bardolino is also the name of the wine that grows on the gentle slopes rising up behind the little town which lies towards the southern end of the eastern shore. This stretch of country was settled back in the Bronze Age. The Romans built a town which developed into the self-governing community of Bardolino in the Middle Ages, when it came under the rule of the House of Scaliger. The Old Town in Bardolino (pop. 6900) is larger than that of other towns along the "Olive Riviera". The shops in the relatively wide lanes that criss-cross each other, stay open until around midnight. But the throngs of people only arrive during the

The beauty of simplicity: San Severo – no pomp and splendour can rival this

summer months. In September, it is already noticeably more peaceful and atmospheric.

SIGHTSEEING

MUSEO DELL'OLIO DI OLIVA

2 km/1.2 mi south of the village of Cisano, near Bardolino, the olive oil museum is the perfect place not just to buy quality oil right from the producer but also to find out in depth how olive oil is manufactured. Don't miss the video show. *Mon–Sat 9am–12.30pm and 2.30pm–7pm, Sun 9am–12.30pm | Via Peschiera 54 | www.museum.it*

MUSEO DEL VINO ●

Gaetano Zeni runs a wine museum on the family estate in which the wine-making process is explained. After you've toured the museum, wines are available for tasting and purchase. *Mid March–Oct daily 9am–12.30pm and 2.30pm–7pm | Via Costabella 9 | www. museodelvino.it*

PIAZZA GIACOMO MATTEOTTI ★

Bardolino's main square is always brimming with life. It is really a relatively wide street that leads from the neo-Classicist parish church San Nicolò down to the lakeside. This is where you'll find a number of bars, cafés and icecream parlours. And this is where the locals and holiday-makers stroll around in the evenings: *fare le vasche* as the Italians call it – "doing lengths".

SAN SEVERO

The small church on the main road was rebuilt in the Romanesque style after the earthquake of 1117. The remains of the previous church, some 300 years older, can still be seen. The faded but largely intact frescos from the 12th century that once covered the whole interior of this harmoniously designed church are particularly beautiful.

VILLAS

Bardolino has an aristocratic face. A walk past these noble residences will take you back to past centuries. The *Villa Guerrieri Rizzardi* with its park (private), which belongs to the winery of the same name, is located in the middle of the old town centre. The *Villa Carrara Bottagisio* features a public park and sits right next to the yellow-coloured *Villa delle Magnolie* (private) and the *Villa delle Rose*, which is also a private estate.

FOOD & DRINK

AL CARDELLINO

The Modena family takes good care of its guests. Mama Rosa makes the pasta by hand, but Papa Aldo is the fish expert. The house also has six small apartments and a pretty garden. *Closed Tue | Via Pralesi 16 | located in Cisano | tel. 04 56 22 90 48 | www.alcardellino.it | Moderate–Expensive*

IL GIARDINO DELLE ESPERIDI

Here, the dishes have something extra special. The starters and main courses are delicious, while the sensation is the chocolate bomb. Booking is essential! *Closed Wed lunchtime and Tue | Via Mameli 1 | tel. 04 56 21 04 77 | www.ilgiardinodelleesperidi.it | Expensive*

LA LOGGIA RAMBALDI

Enjoy tasty pasta, meat and fish on the large terrace in front of the historic Palazzo Rambaldi with a view of the lake. The bar is a popular meeting place. *Closed Tue | Piazza Principe Amedeo 7 | tel. 04 56 21 00 91 | www.laloggiarambaldi.it | Moderate*

DA MEMO

In this quieter corner of the Old Town, sitting outside is just as nice as inside the 16th-century building. One of the specialities is sea bass in a salt crust. *Closed Wed | Piazza Statuto 15 | tel. 04 57 21 01 30 | www.tavernadamemo.com | Moderate*

VILLA CALICANTUS ⊘

In Bardolino's smallest enoteca, Daniele and his wife press organic wines amidst the antique walls. They organize guided tours and generous tastings with home-made and regional products *(30 euros/person)*. Especially romantic: INSIDER TIP the moonlight tasting *Calmasino di Bardolino | Via Concordia 13 | tel. 34 03 66 67 40 | www.villacalicantus.it*

MARCO POLO HIGHLIGHTS

⭐ **Piazza Giacomo Matteotti in Bardolino**
In the evening the piazza on the lake comes alive → p. 52

⭐ **Orto Botanico di Monte Baldo**
At 1200 m/3937 ft extraordinary flora grows with numerous rare species → p. 59

⭐ **Madonna della Corona**
At a height of 774 m/2539 ft, this pilgrimage site is a spectacular oasis of peace – not just for the religious → p. 59

⭐ **Punta San Vigilio**
One of the prettiest corners on the lake with an exclusive beach and a posh restaurant → p. 60

⭐ **Arena di Verona**
The well-preserved amphitheatre is a venue for opera performances and rock concerts → p. 65

SHOPPING

CANTINE LENOTTI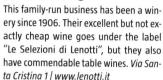

This family-run business has been a winery since 1906. Their excellent but not exactly cheap wine goes under the label "Le Selezioni di Lenotti", but they also have commendable table wines. *Via Santa Cristina 1 | www.lenotti.it*

MARKET

The market – one of the biggest on the lake – is held every Thursday.

LEISURE, SPORTS & BEACHES

No swimming directly in the town itself, but to the north and south of the Old Town there are a number of beaches along the shoreline. The next place to swim nearest to the town centre is Punta Cornicello. The small pebbly beach (free of charge) near Via Ugo Foscolo also has a children's playground. The best way to take a dip in the lake is to jump from a boat, such as a INSIDER TIP historic ketch, which is a fishing boat from the mid-19th century. For over a quarter of a century, Captain Aldo Giarbini has been giving holidaymakers a romantic sailing experience on his four-hour tour far out onto the lake: *Europlan Reservation Service | Mon–Fri 8.30am and 2pm | 35 euros | Via Mirabello15 | tel. 0 456 209 444 | www.europlan.it.*

From Bardolino a superb lake promenade leads both to the north as far as Garda as well as to the south to Lazise. The total length is 10 km/6.2 mi for joggers, hikers and even skaters to enjoy and explore. Don't forget to take bathing costumes, as there are plenty of beaches on the way! A tour, which offers plenty of variation, will take you to Garda in one hour. As you leave the town, the route leaves the lake shore for a short period and heads inland. If you pass the red house, you are heading in the right direction! Some hotels rent bikes, otherwise enquire at the *Bicicaffe (Via Mirabello 3 | tel. 32 82 55 55 52 | www.gardabikerental.it).*

ENTERTAINMENT

HOLLYWOOD

In this legendary dance club, the Simple Minds once rocked the house. House rhythms play in the *Main Room*, while live music can be heard in *Privee Smoking Joy*. Guests can also dine at the *Sinatra Restaurant* next to the pool. Ladies wearing high heels (at least 12 cm) can save the admission charge! *April–Oct Wed and Fri–Sun from 9.30pm | Via Montavoletta 11 | www.hollywood.it*

CONCERTS ●

Every Wednesday in the summer season at 9.30pm, classical music concerts are given on the Piazza Matteotti in front of the church San Nicolò. Classical concerts are held in the church from July until September. *www.filarmonicabardolino.it*

NEW YORK BAR

Remember your dancing shoes! Plenty of nightowls will be delighted – the cult Primo Life Club has become the even cooler New York Bar. Saturdays it gets really lively! *Tue–Sun 9pm–4am | Via Marconi 14*

no. *Via Peschiera 48 | tel. 04 56 22 90 98 | www.camping-cisano.it | Budget*

HOTEL QUATTRO STAGIONI

A large, family-run hotel. Very popular especially since the swimming pool was

The Piazza Matteotti is turned into an open-air concert hall on Wednesday evenings in the summer

WHERE TO STAY

CAESIUS THERME & SPA RESORT

Ayurveda on Lake Garda – you don't believe it? Prepare for an introduction to Indian healing therapy from Dr Pomari and his team at the resort in Cisano. Even dedicated meat-eaters will not miss their steak. *185 rooms | Via Peschiera 3 | tel. 04 57 21 91 00 | www.hotelcaesiusterme. com | Expensive*

CAMPING CISANO

Campers at this site have the choice of several different pools, even though it is right on the lake itself. In Cisano near Bardoli-

built in the garden a few years ago. You can't get more central than this in Bardolino's Old Town. *36 rooms | Borgo Garibaldi 23 | tel. 04 57 21 00 36 | www.hotel4stagio ni.com | Moderate–Expensive*

CAMPING SERENELLA

This campsite offers an informal, friendly atmosphere under olive trees as well as para-sailing sessions at the water ski centre. *Located in Mezzariva 19 | tel. 04 57 21 13 33 | www.camping-serenella.it*

AGRITURISMO TRE COLLINE ⊙

This family-run business is 5 km/3.1 mi further inland from Bardolino. It has a pool, apartments and a small campsite nestled in the vineyards. A solar energy system produces electricity for use on-site and helps generate warm water. On request, you can enjoy tastings of food and local products. An amazing aperitif is the sparkling rosé wine Costa Rosa. *Located in Palù 26 | tel. 04 57 23 52 19 | www. trecollinebardolino.it | Moderate*

LA ZERLA

3 km/1.9 mi away in the hilly countryside, this *agriturismo* is situated in a restored 19th-century residence. The brothers Germano and Ivano Andreoli run the family business with lots of enthusiasm. The rooms are not large, but they're clean. Breakfast not before 8.30am! *15 rooms | located in Ca' Bottura 3a | tel. 04 56 21 12 99 | www.lazerla.it | Budget–Moderate*

INFORMATION

Piazzale Aldo Moro 5 | tel. 04 57 21 00 78 | www.comune.bardolino.vr.it

WHERE TO GO

STRADA DEL VINO
(142–143 C–D 3–5) (*ψ H–J 6–8*)
A route that one person will not really be able to enjoy very much: the driver... The "Wine Route" starts just a little to the north of Bardolino and goes through Affi, Pastrengo and Castelnuovo in the direction of Peschiera. With more than 70 wineries, restaurants and places to stay along the road, you can enjoy, taste and buy all the wine you want. *www. ilbardolino.com/strada-del-vino*

GARDA

(142 C3) (*ψ H6*) **Garda has a population of 4000 and stretches around the wide bay between Punta San Vigilio and the Rocca.**

Its pretty, traffic-free Old Town is popular among locals and tourists alike as a place to stroll. Along the shore lies one café after another. The lanes in the Old Town are quite narrow and the main streets can get very crowded sometimes. However, if you get away from the shops there are still secret corners to be discovered. In the evening things quieten down and you can sit cosily in the cafés along Lungolago Regina Adelaide.

There really lived a real queen once too, Adelaide of Burgundy, who was held prisoner here more than 1000 years ago. As early as 768, Charlemagne had made Garda a county in its own right and from then onwards the lake was named after this town, and not by its earlier Roman name Benacus. On the Rocca above the lake stood a castle where Adelaide was kept captive. Now it is in ruins.

In addition to the Old Town with the many sympathetically restored palazzi, the lush countryside surrounding Garda is a visitor attraction – nature lovers delight in the Mediterranean vegetation. Old monasteries, farms and country houses are tucked away on the hillside slopes and can be explored on longer walking tours.

SIGHTSEEING

ROCCA DI GARDA

The Rocca di Garda is a hill that presides about 200 m/656 ft over the eastern shore. From the top, you can enjoy the amazing view over Garda and Punta San Vigilio. Although the area is now covered in forest, a thousand years ago it was the site of a fortress in which Queen Adelheid was held captive. All that is left of the castle today is a few stones. A well-marked trail leads up to the castle from behind the Santa Maria Maggiore church.

SANTA MARIA MAGGIORE

Garda's parish church is outside the original town walls. It is presumed that the earlier structure on the site, built by the Lombards in the 8th century, was the fortress chapel, as the site is directly below the Rocca. The INSIDER TIP 15th-century cloisters are well worth seeing. *Piazzale Roma*

VILLA ALBERTINI

The dark red villa at the northern town entrance, with its distinctive crenellated Ghibelline-style towers, cannot be missed. It can only be viewed from the outside.

gourmet dishes which are pricey. Those looking for a memorable evening in an exclusive setting – shorts and sandals are not desired – will definitely be happy here. Closed all day Tue, Wed lunchtime, July/Aug Tue and Thu at lunchtime | *Via Val Mora 57 | tel. 04 57 25 57 80 | www. ristoranteaibeati.com | Expensive*

RISTORANTE GIARDINETTO

Slightly away from the hustle and bustle although directly on the lake, this is the best place for fish dishes such as spaghetti with lobster. *Daily | Lungolago Regina Adelaide 27 | tel. 04 57 25 50 51 | www. hotel-giardinetto.it | Expensive*

FOOD & DRINK

AI BEATI

The restaurant is at the top of the hill, reached after turning left off the road to Costermano. The location is stunning and popular with trendy guests who enjoy

SHOPPING

INSIDER TIP LA BOTTEGA DELLA PASTA

This shop is all about pasta: what is normal for Italian housewives is a mini-attraction for many tourists – a shop with exclusively fresh home-made pasta.

The Villa Albertini, with its distinctive battlements, lies on the outskirts of Garda

Among the specialities of the store in Costermano, which is 4 km/2.5 mi to the east, are various stuffed tortellini and *tortelli. Via San Giuseppe Artigiano 2b*

COOPERATIVA FRA PESCATORI ●
Fresh fish can be bought from the local fishing cooperative. *Daily 6.30am–12.30pm | Via San Bernardo 79*

MARKET
Every Friday morning there is a market on *Lungolago Regina Adelaide*.

LEISURE, SPORTS & BEACH

Just to the north of Garda there is a long, narrow pebbly beach which is the favourite haunt of local youths. No entrance charge, but there are hardly any parking spaces. In Marciaga, 2 km/1.2 mi to the north, you will find a very well-maintained 18-hole golf course and a large climbing area with many light routes rated up to 6a nestled in the hills covered with vineyards and olive trees.

ENTERTAINMENT

ART CAFE
Exhibitions are held in cooperation with the Cerchio Aperto Culture Association at this special location as well as the occasional open-air concert organised in conjunction with the restaurant Giardino delle Rane. *Daily 7am–midnight | Piazza Calderini 1*

PAPILLON
Live music is played in this music bar well into the night – but not on a regular basis. *Wed–Mon 7.30pm–3am | Via delle Antiche Mura 22*

WHERE TO STAY

PICCOLO HOTEL
A perfect location in the Old Town with a welcoming ambiance and exceptionally good value. Just make yourself at home here! *9 rooms | Piazza Catullo 11/12 | tel. 04 57 25 52 56 | www.piccolohotelgarda. it | Budget*

Numerous cafés await visitors along the small harbour in Garda

TOBAGO WELLNESS-HOTEL ⊘

This modern spa hotel with many designer elements has been awarded the "eco-label"; it also has a large heated outdoor pool. *18 rooms | Via della Pace 1 | tel. 04 57 25 63 40 | www.hoteltobago.it | Expensive*

TRE CORONE

This hotel was opened in 1860 as a coaching inn and is mentioned in the 1895 edition of Baedeker's. Today it is a standard-category hotel whose trump card is the view of the lake from many of its rooms. *26 rooms | Lungolago Regina Adelaide 54 | tel. 04 57 25 53 36 | www.hoteltrecorone.it | Moderate*

INFORMATION

Piazza Donatori di Sangue 1 | tel. 04 57 25 58 24

WHERE TO GO

EREMO SAN GIORGIO ⊘
(142 C3) (*Ⓜ H6*)

Even atheists will find peace here: the Camaldolese hermitage has been a retreat since the 17th century for those in need, from monks to farmers. Nowadays, it is also a place of rest for anybody who wishes to escape the hectic pace of city life. You can request single rooms for overnight stays. In the monastery shop homemade organic products are on sale – the honey, liqueurs and syrups are mouthwateringly good. *Tel. 04 57 21 13 90 | www.eremosangiorgio.it*

ROCK ENGRAVINGS
(142 B–C3) (*Ⓜ H6*)

Please note, engravings were carved into the rock face here – and that was already 3000 years ago. Presumably, the engravings were left by shepherds who left their artistic mark here at the foot of Monte Baldo and especially on Monte Luppia in the bay of Garda and engraved ships, riders, warriors and lances. From Garda, there is a pathway with routemarkers and information boards.

WAR GRAVES (142 C3) (*Ⓜ H6*)

It is sad, but true: further inland near Garda and south of Costermano is the *Cimitero Militare Tedesco*, the largest military cemetery for German soldiers in Italy. Almost 22,000 Germans are laid to rest here. They were killed in North Italy during World War Two. A controversy erupted when it became known that not only victims, but also perpetrators were buried at the cemetery. The following notice is therefore displayed on an information board: "At this cemetery lie the mortal remains of those who were also actively responsible for war crimes. Their crimes will always be a warning to us."

MADONNA DELLA CORONA ★
(143 E2) (*Ⓜ J5*)

One of the most picturesque and spectacular sites on Lake Garda is this pilgrimage church 774 m/2539 ft above the Adige Valley. In the 15th century, the church was built right into the cliff that towers above the village of Spiazzi. A hermitage had already been established here in the late 12th century. If you are up for it, you can hike two hours up the steep pilgrimage path from Brentino on the eastern side of Monte Baldo to the santuario. The easiest way to get to the church is by taking Bus No. 167, which links Garda and Spiazzi. *www.madonnadellacorona.it*

ORTO BOTANICO DI MONTE BALDO ★
(143 E1) (*Ⓜ J5*)

Over 600 species of plants grow on the slopes of Monte Baldo, including a number of botanical rarities. Many refer to these botanical gardens, which first opened in 1989, as the "Garden of Europe". At a height of 1200 m/3937 ft near Novezzina, it houses an extraordinary collection of plants, many of which are endemic to the area. The gardens can be reached by heading out to Caprino Veronese, then via Spiazzi, Ferrara di Monte Baldo and Novezzina (in total approx. 20 km/12.4 mi). *Opens about 2 weeks after the snow melts until the onset of winter, daily, 9am–sunset | tours by appointment, tel. 04 56 24 72 88 | www.orto botanicomontebaldo.org*

PUNTA SAN VIGILIO ⭐
(142 B3) *(ⵁ G6)*

A peninsula lying immediately to the west of Garda. An extensive olive grove follows the curve of the lovely bay – the Baia delle Sirene *(www.parcobaiadellesi rene.it)*, where you can bathe – at a price: *entrance fee 12 euros*. There is also a children's activity programme *(5 euros)*. In 1540, Michele Sanmicheli – an accomplished builder of fortresses – constructed the *Villa Guarienti-Brenzone* on the peninsula. Those who can afford it stay at the *Locanda San Vigilio (7 rooms | tel. 04 57 25 66 88 | www.locanda-sanvi gilio.it | Expensive)*. Those on a more modest budget can at least enjoy a cappuccino or a campari here.

SAN ZENO DI MONTAGNA ⵁ
(142 C2) *(ⵁ H5)*

A beautiful ⵁ panoramic route takes you from Garda via Costermano to San Zeno, 25 km/15.5 mi to the north. The small village is about 560 m/1837 ft high up the mountain and is a winter sports resort with a stunning view of the lake. In summer, nature lovers are drawn here, while gourmets arrive in the autumn. Then, the chestnuts are ripe and feature as starters, side dishes or as desserts. Treat yourself to the mouthwatering specialities at the INSIDER TIP *Taverna Kus (Nov–Feb, closed Mon–Wed | quarter Castello 14 | tel. 04 57 28 56 67 | www.ris toranteveronatavernakus.it | Moderate– Budget):* – and sample the chestnuts. A celebration of exceptional cuisine.

One night in the Locanda San Vigilio: treat yourself! Too pricey? OK, so just a cappuccino...

Typical cuisine is also available at the ☙ *Agriturismo La Part (daily) | quarter La Pora | tel. 04 57 28 52 77 | www.agritur ismolapart.com | Budget)* with three guest rooms and farm shop. Accommodation e. g. in Hotel Sole (*Via Cá Schena 1 | tel. 04 57 28 50 01 | www.albergosole. com | Budget).*

LAZISE

(142 C4) (*ṁ H7*) The little village almost seems as if it wants to ward off visitors: the 14th-century fortified walls around the Old Town of Lazise (pop. 7000) are still fully intact, and you can only enter through three gateways.

It is significantly quieter here than in any of the other places on the east shore and this makes the pretty old place with its promenade, the unusually large *Piazza* Vittorio Emanuele, all the more attractive. Lazise was an important trading post under Venetian rule. A visible reminder of that time can be seen in the customs house at the harbour, from where Venice kept a watch on the trading of goods on the lake.

SIGHTSEEING

SAN NICOLÒ

Pause, light a candle and admire the beautifully restored frescoes... The small church is right on the harbourside and is worth a detour.

SCALIGER CASTLE

The castle dates from the 12th and 13th centuries and can only be viewed from the outside, as it is a private residence. Scaliger Castle was fortified to protect the strategically important Lazise harbour.

TOWN WALL

The fact that a wall was built around almost all of the Old Town of Lazise has an historical explanation: Venice continually strengthened its outposts on Lake Garda against attacks from Milan.

FOOD & DRINK

AL CASTELLO

Sitting in a large inner courtyard, right next to the town wall, guests can enjoy grilled trout, spaghetti with clams and other specialities. *Closed Thu lunchtime | Via Porta del Lion 8 | tel. 04 56 47 10 22 | www.famigliabozzini.it | Moderate*

CLASSIQUE ☙

One of the most beautifully situated restaurants on the lake in an historical villa from the 19th century slightly above the lakeside promenade. You'll find the view across the lake quite breath-taking. Inside, marvel at the floor mosaics. For those who want to wake up to a view over the lake, there are also seven wonderfully comfortable rooms. *Daily |*

Via Albarello 33 | tel. 04 57 58 02 70 | www.ristoclassique.it | Moderate

CORTE OLIVO

Pizza and co. can be enjoyed here in one of the most beautiful courtyards just inside the town walls. *Closed Mon | Corso Cangrande 22 | tel. 04 57 58 13 47 | Moderate*

LA FORGIA

The former smithy is now a fish restaurant where the chef de cuisine, Omero Rossignoli, has specialised in all types of seafood – grilled, of course. After all, an open fire is always to be found in a forge. *Closed Mon | Via Calle 1 | tel. 04 56 47 03 72 | Expensive*

GEM'S BREW PUB

The self-brewed, natural and unfiltered beer in this pub & pizzeria goes down well. It is popular among locals who like to sit at the rustic wooden tables outside or drink their beer in traditional pub style inside. *Daily | Located in Praleor 25 | tel. 04 56 47 11 44 | www.gemsbrewpub.it | Budget*

ALLA GROTTA

Connoisseurs appreciate the restaurant's exceptional and inspired (fish)-cuisine by the small harbour for boats. The adjoining hotel is simple with twelve functional rooms with pleasant decor. *Closed Tue | Via Francesco Fontana 8 | tel. 04 57 58 00 35 | www.allagrotta.it | Moderate*

SHOPPING

ENOTECA L'ARTE DEL BERE

"The Art of Drinking" is the name of this *enoteca*, based on the notion that life is too short to drink poor wine. The extensive list of wines proves how appropriate the name is. *Via Cansignorio 10 | www.artedelbere.com*

MARKET

A market is held every Wednesday morning on *Lungolago Marconi*.

LEISURE, SPORTS & BEACH

Patrick Planatscher, a native of South Tyrol, organises water sports activities such as wake boarding and fly boarding and fun programmes for children over 5 at *Gardawake (Via Pra del Principe | tel. 34 94 07 60 04 | www.gardawake.com)*

ENTERTAINMENT

The evenings in Lazise are a quiet affair. Just sit on the large *Piazza Vittorio Emanuele* and enjoy a glass of wine. The local (surfers) scene enjoys meeting for aperitifs at the *Paparazzi Lounge Cafè (Via Gardesana 52)*.

WHERE TO STAY

CANGRANDE GARNI

Guests staying in this elegant palazzo next to the medieval walls in the centre of Lazise can soak up the peace and quiet. Suite 119 has a beautiful roof terrace with a view of the lake. *23 rooms | Corso Cangrande 16 | tel. 04 56 47 04 10 | www.cangrandehotel.it | Expensive*

IL GIARDINO DEGLI ULIVI

All rooms in this *agriturismo* guesthouse have lovely views of the lake. There is also an "Agricamping" with ten pitches, a small swimming pool and homemade olive oil. *6 rooms | Via Fossalta 12 | tel. 34 74 00 15 45 | www.ilgiardinodegliulivi.info | Budget–Moderate*

PIANI DI CLODIA

This four-star campsite with three pools also has several lodges, flats (*Budget–*

Moderate) and luxury tents to rent as well as pitches for dormobil and caravans. *Via Fossalta 42 | tel. 04 57 59 04 56 | www.pianidiclodia.it*

Mincio. Just before reaching the village, you pass over the *Ponte Visconteo*, a gigantic stone bridge that was designed as a dam. Here, on the third Tuesday in June

Unusually large for a small town on the lake: Piazza Vittorio Emanuele in Lazise

AGRITURISMO LE TESE

This peacefully situated property, surrounded by vineyards, is particularly welcoming. Homemade cake is served for breakfast. *3 flats | located in Tese 2 | Colà di Lazise | tel. 04 57 59 53 14 | www. letese.it | Moderate*

INFORMATION

Piazzetta Partenio 5 | tel. 36 64 22 30 17 | iatlazise@provinciadiveronaturismo.it

WHERE TO GO

BORGHETTO DI VALEGGIO SUL MINCIO (0) *(ɱ 0)*

A good 30-min drive along the Mincio will lead you to Borghetto di Valeggio sul

the village of Valeggio celebrates its tortellini festival on a long table measuring about 600 m/1969 ft.

Pasta fans can also sample the village's culinary speciality in the excellent restaurants. Try the popular *Antica Locanda Mincio (Closed Wed/Thu | Via Michelangelo Buonarroti 12 | tel. 04 57 95 00 59 | www.anticalocandamincio.it | Expensive)*. The pasta is simply sublime at *Alla Borsa (Closed Tue/Wed | Via Goito 2 | tel. 04 57 95 00 93 | www.ristoranteborsa.it | Moderate–Expensive)*. If you have trouble deciding, try the *tris* – INSIDER TIP the three most delicious tortellini varieties! Pasta and tortellini, which are incredibly light and delicate, are available to take away at *Pastificio Remelli (Via Alessandro Sala 24 | www.pastificioremelli.it)*.

GARDEN CENTRE FLOVER IN BUSSOLENGO ●

If the weather isn't fine, the Garden Centre *Flover (daily 9am–7.30pm | Via Pastrengo 14–16 | www.flover.it)* in Bussolengo is a welcome alternative to a walk in the rain. All year round inspiring exhibitions and workshops on the theme of home

Bursting with flowers and a green idyll: Parco Giardino Sigurtà

and garden are held. The highlight in December is the Father Christmas village.

PARCO GIARDINO SIGURTÀ (0) *(m 0)*

The 50-ha/124-acre garden and nature park, which is about 14 km/8.7 mi to the south, can be explored on foot, by bicycle or with a miniature train. From mid-March the tulips in bloom are fabulous when about 1 million tulip bulbs from 300 different varieties are on display for INSIDER TIP *Tulipanomia*. *Mid-March–Oct daily 9am–6pm (March and Oct until 5pm) | www.sigurta.it*

PARCO TERMALE DEL GARDA ● (142 C5) *(m H7)*

You can enjoy the waters in the hot spring baths in *Colà di Lazise* – with a temperature of 37 ˚C/99 ˚F – INSIDER TIP and the baths are open until late. Then, it gets quieter and the baths have romantic lighting. Take a picnic and soak up the atmosphere in the park beneath the ancient trees! Hot water bubbles out of the ground further inland. You can bathe in the waters in the hot-spring baths, which have a temperature of 37 °C/98.6 °F and are open until late. Concerts are held in the evenings in the park with its ancient trees and in the Villa dei Cedri. *www.villadeicedri.it*

PESCHIERA DEL GARDA (142 C5) *(m H8)*

Peschiera is a further 8 km/5 mi to the south at the southern-most point of Lake Garda. This is where the water from the lake, fed by the Sarca in Riva in the north, flows out as the Mincio in the south towards the Po and ultimately into the Adriatic Sea. The Mincio forms the boundary between the regions of Veneto and Lombardy. From 1516 onwards, Peschiera came under the rule of Venice. The Austro-Venetian fortresses are particularly worth visiting. A lot of trains on the Milan–Venice route stop at Peschiera. The history of fishing on Lake Garda can be traced in the *Museo della Pesca e della Tradizione (Sat/Sun 10am–12.30pm and 4pm–6.30pm | www.amicidelgondolin.it)* in the former Habsburg barracks on the left-hand side of the Canale di Mezzo. It includes photographs, fishing equipment and information on the geology of the lake. Anyone who fancies a day away from the lake and a gentle bike ride can follow the course of the Muncio from Peschiera to Mantova – which is flat all the way. Almost 40 km/24.9 mi along a cycle path. For the return journey you can even take the train. If you don't have your own bike with you, you can rent one from *Noleggio Bici (Via Venezia 21 | tel. 34 74 56 38 62 | www.noleggio-bici-peschiera.it).*

A stroll around the narrow streets in the Old Town is also a delight. If you want to soak up its tranquillity head for the *Gelateria Centrale (Via Dante 21)* and take a table overlooking the Mincio canal. "From the field to the table" is the motto of the ◉ *farmer's market (Thu mornings | Piazza Generale Dalla Chiesa), 3 km/1.9 mi away in San Benedetto di Lugana,* where local farmers sell their seasonal produce: fresh, from just around the corner, sold directly to the customer – fair trade on an everyday scale!

Accommodation is available in *Bell'-Arrivo (27 rooms | Piazzetta Benacense 2 | tel. 04 56 40 13 22 | www.hotelbellarrivo.it | Moderate).* A relaxed restaurant by the lake is the *Vecchio Mulino (daily | Strada Bergamini 14 | tel. 04 59 23 30 82 | www.vecchiomulinobeach.com | Moderate),* a beach bar with restaurant (also offers vegan food). The small INSIDER TIP *Osteria Goto* on the edge of the Old Town is recommended *(Closed Thu | tel. 04 57 55 01 08 | Moderate).* The chefs produce excellent pasta dishes – and it has become a popular place to eat among young locals.

VERON ● (143 F5) *(ⓜ K8)*

Whoever has had enough of the holiday atmosphere and lying on beaches, and who fancies a bit of city life, should head off for Verona. The city, just 25 km/15.5 mi to the east (pop. 264,000) has a whole range of sites of immense cultural importance as well as a pedestrian precinct where you can shop till you drop. But before you leap in your car and set off for Verona – how about taking the train? From the south of the lake this is no problem at all – and from many other towns on Lake Garda there is a regular bus service to Verona. The *Verona Card* (available in museums and tobacco shops, *www.veronacard.it)* is a combined ticket for entrance to museums, churches and major sites of interest as well as for travelling on public transport within the city of Verona; a one-day ticket costs 18 euros. Due to its position at the end of the route that crosses the Alps via the lowest mountain pass, the Brenner, Verona developed into an important city under the Romans. And Verona's most famous structure dates from Roman times: the ★ *Arena di Verona (Mon 1.30pm–7.30 pm, Tue–Sun 8.30am–7.30pm | on days*

CITY **WHERE TO START?**

Piazza Bra: The large square where the arena is, makes the perfect starting point for a tour of the city. It's best to arrive by train and it's only a ten-minute walk from Porta Nuova station to the city centre. If you prefer to travel by car, there is a multi-storey car park on Piazza Citadella close to the arena.

If you don't want to go to the opera, you can still visit the arena in Verona during the day

operas are performed 9am–3.30pm | Piazza Bra | ticket office: Via Dietro Anfiteatro 6b | tel. opera festival 04 58 00 51 51 | www.arena.it). Start your tour of the city from here. The Roman amphitheatre, dating from the 1st century AD, was badly damaged by an earthquake in the 12th century. Only four arches, which were part of the outer wall are still standing today. The arena can be visited during the day, but it is best seen in its full glory on one of its famous opera evenings. The première of these performances was Verdi's Aida to commemorate the composer's 100th birthday in August 1913.

The Via Roma from the Arena will take you to the *Castelvecchio (Tue–Sun 8.30am–7.30pm, Mon 1.30pm–7.30pm).* The brick-red castle of 1534 is the largest building erected under the Scaligers. Temporary exhibitions are held within its walls. Walking upriver along the upper bank next to the Adige you will reach the Piaz-za Portichetti. This is a slight detour, but it leads to *San Zeno Maggiore* – the church best loved by the locals – with its stunning portal decorated with 48 bronze panels. Detailed information on Verona's churches can be found under *www.chieseverona.it.*

Now take the same route back to the arena. Fancy a refreshing drink in the main square? Drop in at the Piazza Bra in *Via Mazzini*, Verona's main shopping street. This leads to the *Piazza delle Erbe*, where a fruit and vegetable market is held every day in the former Roman forum.

Our tour continues via the *Piazza dei Signori* and the *Scavi Scaligeri* where photography exhibitions, organised by the Centro Internazionale di Fotografia, are regularly held in the excavated areas. The Scaliger tombs are nearby: above the Gothic graves of the former ruling dynasty are life-sized equestrian statues of family members.

At Via Cappello 23 close by, there is an unremarkable 14th-century house that virtually ever visitor to Verona has to have seen – whether or not they have ever read Shakespeare's famous Romeo and Juliet or not. *Casa Capuleti* is the official name of Juliet's house *(Mon 1.30pm–7.30pm, Tue–Sun 8.30am–7.30pm)*. Touching the right-hand breast of the statue of Juliet in the inner courtyard is supposed to bring good luck! The lovers' balcony – which appears on virtually every postcard of Verona – was, however, only added to the façade in 1940.

The *Osteria Sgarzarie (Closed Tue in the winter | Corte Sgarzarie 14a | tel. 04 58 00 03 12 | www.osteriasgarzarie.com | Moderate)* not far from the Piazza Erbe, is a good place to eat, far from the madding crowd. Veronese cuisine can be enjoyed in the *Trattoria Tre Marchetti (closed Mon lunchtime and all day Sun, closed Mon only in July/Aug | Vicolo Tre Marchetti 19b | tel. 04 58 03 04 63 | www.tremarchetti.it | Expensive)*. The restaurant is one of the best the city has to offer and has received numerous awards. For those staying the night: the small, cosy *B & B Vicolo 22 (3 rooms | Via Santa Caterina 22 | tel. 34 82 71 93 93 | Moderate)* is located right in the centre. The proprietors are friendly and take pains to ensure the well-being of their guests. Information: *Piazza Bra | tel. 04 58 06 86 80 | www.tourism.verona.it*

TORRI DEL BENACO

(142 C2) *(ɰ H6)* **The best way to get to Torri del Benaco (pop. 2900) is to take the ferry from Maderno. It is a very practical way to travel – unless one wants to drive half way round the lake to visit the opposite shore.**

From the lake it is clear to see how dominantly ● Scaliger Castle overlooks the town. In 1383 the Scaliger ruler Antonio della Scala, had the fortress, which dates from the 9th century, turned into a residence. During renovation work in the 20th century a pink coloured marble plaque was discovered in the castle, which bears a carved relief of the Scaliger coat-of-arms – a "scale" in the form of a ladder with five rungs, now on show in the museum. Today, the castle is a INSIDER TIP best-kept secret among wedding couples because you can get married in a civil ceremony. The tower with its view of the lake or the Limonaie are particularly romantic locations onsite (more info about weddings: *www.torri-del-benaco.net*).

Torri del Benaco is one of the quieter places on the east shore and is not nearly as overrun as its neighbours Garda or even Bardolino. Probably the most picturesque harbour on the lake stretches right into the town itself and in the oval-shaped harbour small, brightly coloured fishing boats bob up and down. There are just a few narrow lanes that lead away from the harbour basin and there is often surprisingly little going on. The countryside beyond Torri del Benaco is not as steep as elsewhere, Monte Baldo is slightly further away here from the lake.

SIGHTSEEING

MUSEO DEL CASTELLO SCALIGERO

In the folk museum in Scaliger Castle a good insight can be gained of how the people on Lake Garda used to live before the tourists came, earning their living primarily from fishing and the olive industry. The displays on boat building and the rock engravings in the area are particularly interesting. Visitors to the museum can also see a

INSIDER TIP ▶ **lemon glasshouse** built in 1760 – the only one on the east shore that is still being used. *Mid-June–mid-Sept daily 9.30am–1pm and 4.30pm–7.30pm, April–mid-Jun and mid-Sept–Oct 9.30am–12.30pm and 2.30pm–6pm except Mon | Viale Fratelli Lavanda 2 | www.museodelcastelloditorridelbenaco.it*

FOOD & DRINK

LE GEMME DI ARTEMISIA

Have you always wondered how to fill tortellini yourself? Or how top Italian chefs make risotto with truffles? If yes, then you should sign up for a cooking lesson with Chef Andrea Messini from Le

An old palazzo right on the harbour with deliciously prepared fresh fish: Albergo Gardesana

SANTI PIETRO E PAOLO

The large church organ of 1744, which is still used, is an unusual one to find in Italy. Another unusual feature in this Baroque church is the bronze statue of the priest Giuseppe Nascimbeni, who was beatified in 1988. Nascimbeni founded the charitable convent in Torri. *www.parrochiaditorridelbenaco.it*

SANTISSIMA TRINITÀ

Small but beautiful – the little church by the harbour originates from the 14th century and accommodates renovated frescos by the School of Giotto, the Renaissance painter in Northern Italy.

Gemme di Artemisia (available on request). Alongside his restaurant business – only a single table with a surprise menu – in Albisano, he also shares the secrets of his craft with those who are interested. *Closed lunchtimes | Albisano | Via Corrubio 18 | tel. 0452428622 | www.legemmediartemisia.it | Expensive*

ALLA GROTTA

You cannot get closer to the lake: with the sound of babbling water on the small terrace above the lake, the fish and pizza taste three times as good! *Daily | Corso Dante Alighieri 61 | tel. 3477606000 | Moderate*

TRATTORIA LONCRINO

Only 500 m/1640 ft from the centre, in Loncrino, you can tuck into local food served in a relaxed atmosphere enjoy a view of the lake from the 🌿 terrace. *Daily | Via Pirandello 10 | located in Loncrino | tel. 04 56 29 00 18 | Budget–Moderate*

SHOPPING

ARTS & CRAFTS MARKET

At the height of summer, artists and craftspeople set up their stalls in the old town centre every Thursday from 8pm until 11.30pm.

MARKET

Every Monday morning a market is held on the road along the shore.

LEISURE & BEACH

A long beach (free access) can be found at the southern end of the village; a few willow trees offer a little shade. *Tra gli Olivi i Tesori di Torri del Benaco,* "Between the olive trees, the treasures of Torri" is the name of a path that will take you to nine little churches in the area.

ENTERTAINMENT

Film showings take place in the new theatre in summer.

WHERE TO STAY

ALBERGO RISTORANTE GARDESANA

There is no more beautiful place to stay in Torri than here – that's if you can do without a pool. As a reward you sleep in the Palazzo dei Capitani, originally built as the town-hall, directly on the harbourside. *34 rooms | Piazza Calderini 5 | tel. 04 57 22 54 11 | www.gardesana.eu | Expensive*

AI SALICI

This no-frills campsite is on the other side of the road from the lake, but there is a tunnel leading to the beach. *Via Pai di Sotto 97 | tel. 04 57 26 01 96*

VILLA SUSY

The small, family-run hotel is just a few minutes' walk from the heart of the Old Town, down on the lake, which has a pleasant beach. Book a room with a lake view – on the other side the traffic streams along the Gardesana. *14 rooms | Via Gardesana 119 | tel. 04 57 22 59 65 | Moderate*

INFORMATION

Via Gardesana 5 | tel. 04 57 22 51 20 | www.torridelbenaco.de

WHERE TO GO

ALBISANO 🌿 (142 C2) (*ØØ H6*)

A waymarked footpath (pretty steep) will take you up to the village, which 2 km/1.2 mi up from Torri clings onto the ridge of Monte Baldo, in approximately 45 minutes. But then you'll be gasping for breath anyway when you get to the top – the view from the terrace of the parish church is breathtakingly beautiful.

INSIDER TIP GROTTA TANELLA
(142 C1–2) (*ØØ H5*)

Head 6 km/3.7 mi to the north to Pai di Sopra for the caves "Grotta Tanella" which lead about 400 m/1312 ft deep into the rocky cliff of Monte Baldo and admire the stalactites and stalagmites – a genuine alternative to the usual beach routine. The guided tour is accompanied by experts of the association *Biosphaera (Piazza San Marco | tel. 34 07 66 11 16 | www.biosphaera.it)*.

SOUTH SHORE

While the north shore is more fjord-like, the south shore is lovely and has extensive and pleasant beaches, surrounded by the undulating glacial landscape and vineyards.

The atmosphere in the south is more Mediterranean and Latin. Instead of Alpine mountains, further inland the hillsides are more undulating. This is where the famous Lugana white wine is pressed. Sirmione and Desenzano are the main tourist attractions. During the summer months, the historic town of Sirmione is almost overcrowded with tourists. But in the evenings when the throngs of day-trippers have departed, it becomes peaceful and pleasant in the maze of lanes. The lively "metropolis" Desenzano is the biggest town on the lake. It is less affected by crowds and is ideal for shopping with a lovely jetty in the harbour.

DESENZANO

(141 D5) *(⚏ F7)* **While other towns may have nicer lakeside promenades, Desenzano's harbour wall is hard to beat. It comes as no surprise that it is not just the fishermen who can be found here when the sun goes down – this romantic spot is a favourite among couples, too.**

Desenzano, with a population of just under 28,000, is the largest town on Lake Garda – and, to be more precise, the oldest. When the glaciers started to retreat northwards at the end of the last Ice Age that carved out the basin of today's Lake

Photo: Harbour in Desenzano

Roman remains, shops and nightlife: in Desenzano and Sirmione you'll find yourself immersed in the Italian way of life

Garda, this was the first area around the lake that could support life. The Romans also settled here as the excavation of a villa with beautiful floor mosaics from the 3rd century goes to prove. Desenzano was repeatedly the object of foreign rulers' desire, as its harbour at the southern end of the lake was a strategically important hub for trade.

What it lacks in the way of beaches it makes up for with its bustling street life. Good shops and window displays can be found in the extensive pedestrian precinct,

and you can easily spend hours over a cappuccino or two in one of the cafés on the Piazza Matteotti just watching the comings and goings. And in the evenings, it's very hard finding a place in any of the bars around the old harbour.

On Friday and Saturday evenings, right up until midnight, the narrow pedestrianised streets are completely chock-a-block. Young people from all around meet up here, styled through and through and ready for a flirt. After strolling around they head off for the discos in the vicinity.

SIGHTSEEING

CASTELLO ✂

It is worth taking INSIDERTIP a short stroll upwards to Desenzano Castle for the view, as there are few other possibilities to enjoy such as far-reaching vista of the surrounding countryside from anywhere else along the flat south shore.

MUSEO CIVICO ARCHEOLOGICO GIOVANNI RAMBOTTI

The museum is housed in a 15th-century cloister – that alone is worth seeing. One of the most interesting exhibits is a 2 m-/6.6 ft-long oak plough dating from the 2nd millenium (!) BC. *Tue/Wed 9am–1pm, Thu/Fri 3pm–7pm, Sat/Sun 2.30pm–7pm | Via Tommaso Dal Molin 7c | in the*

At aperitif time, it is a tradition to stroll about the streets in Desenzano, too

June–Sept Tue–Sun 9.30am–12.30pm and 4.30pm–7.30pm, April/May and Oct 10am–12.30pm and 3pm–6pm

LUNGOLAGO CESARE BATTISTI

Walking along the lakeside promenade you have a lovely view across the water – and of the motorboats that sometimes race past at an incredible speed. But they are nothing compared to what Francesco Agello did here back in 1934: he set up a new record by reaching a speed of 709 km/h (440 mph)! A sculpture in the Mayer & Splendid hotel commemorates this deed.

Chiostro di Santa Maria de Senioribus | www.onde.net/desenzano/citta/museo

SANTA MARIA MADDALENA

Church lovers will be impressed! Inside dates entirely from the 16th-century Renaissance period and almost resembles an art gallery. "The Last Supper" by Giambattista Tiepolo (1696–1770) is well worth seeing.

VILLA ROMANA

The carpenter Emanuele Zamboni was probably less enthusiastic about history after he discovered the remains of a 1075 ft² Roman yeoman's dwelling when digging the foundations for his house in 1921. The floor mosaics are especially interesting, as is the hypocaust, the Roman equivalent to today's under-floor heating. *Tue–Sun 8.30am–7pm (in winter until 5pm) | Via Crocefisso 22*

FOOD & DRINK

RISTORANTE COLOMBA

A bit of retro by the lake: a wonderful spot for a delicious evening meal. Try the Tiramisu, it's wonderfully creamy! *Daily | Vicolo dell'Interdetto 16 (Via Porto Vecchio) | tel. 03 09 14 37 01 | www.ristorantecolomba.it | Budget–Expensive*

OSTERIA LA CONTRADA

This elegant osteria furnished with antiques has an emphasis on Lombard and Venetian cuisine such as *risotto all'amarone* (an excellent, full-bodied red wine) or *baccalá* (dried cod) *alla vicentina*. *Closed Wed | Via Bagatta 12 | tel. 03 09 14 25 14 | Expensive*

DE' CORTE POZZI

This enoteca has moved into the courtyard of a palazzo. And if you get hungry when sampling the wines, you can also eat here – such as grilled steak. *Daily | Via Stretta Castello 3 | tel. 03 09 14 17 56 | Moderate*

KAPPERI

A modern restaurant with a pretty garden in which the atmosphere is lively and dynamic. Great food, including pizzas that attract a younger crowd. Wide selection of gluten-free dishes. *Closed Mon | Via Nazario Sauro 7 | tel. 03 09 99 18 93 | www.kapperi.eu | Moderate–Expensive*

SQUARE 16

The chic, relaxing eatery opposite the moorings has a good view from the 🌿 restaurant on the second floor. The ground floor is the haunt of a younger crowd who sip their wine until the early hours. *Closed at lunchtime except Sat/Sun | Piazza Matteotti 16 | tel. 03 02 07 79 27 | square16.playrestaurant.tv | Moderate–Expensive*

GELATERIA VIVALDI ⊛

The ice cream here is the best in town – and only cream and milk from organic farms is used. The pistacchio is amazing! *Piazza Matteotti 9*

SHOPPING

PASTICCERIA DOLCE MARILA

If you easily give into temptation, you shouldn't walk past here: admire the gateaux, little cakes, savoury snacks and pastries, each more alluring than the next. There is also a good selection of gluten-free treats. *Via Giuseppe di Vittorio 96*

⭐ **Grotte di Catullo in Sirmione**
Not caves but the remains of a Roman villa with a view of the lake → p. 76

⭐ **Rocca Scaligera in Sirmione**
A moated castle on Roman foundations rises out the lake like in a fairy tale → p. 76

⭐ **Lido delle Bionde in Sirmione**
A large pebbly beach with a café and paddle-boats, where the water is not deep → p. 78

MARCO POLO HIGHLIGHTS

FRANTOIO DI MONTECROCE
Fresh and (cold) pressed olive oil can be bought at this *azienda agricola* in Montecroce. *Viale Ettore Andreis 84 | www.frantoiomontecroce.it*

IL LEONE DI LONATO
120 shops can be found in this shopping centre 2 km/1.2 mi from the Desenzano motorway exit in the direction of Castiglione delle Stiviere. *Daily 9am–10pm | www.illeonedilonato.com*

MARKETS
A market is held every Tuesday morning on the road next to the lake and a farmers' market is set up every Thursday morning on Piazza Garibaldi. Every first Sunday of the month – except in January and August – the old town hosts *an antiques market.*

LEISURE, SPORTS & BEACHES

The *Lido di Padenghe* has a large pebbly and sandy beach and is free of charge; the *Lido di Lonato* also costs nothing and has very fine pebbles. Between Desenzano and the Sirmione peninsula, as well as to the north along the hilly Valtenesi, you will come across a number of other places to swim or sunbathe. If you would like to explore the countryside in peace, rent a bike and follow the suggested Strada dei Vini routes through the vineyards of Lugana or Valtenesi (short.travel/gar1).

ENTERTAINMENT

For those infected by Saturday-night-fever there's no avoiding Desenzano – the town is *the* nightlife centre on the lake.

COCO BEACH CLUB
For a bit of Miami flair on Lake Garda, locals and tourists alike flock to the fine sand beach at Lido di Lonato to party the night away in style. *Wed and Fri–Sun from 6pm | Via Catullo 5 | www.cocobeachclub.com*

GELATERIA CRISTALLO
A popular bar in the evening – perhaps because of the swing seats, from which you get a good view of the nightlife around the old harbour. *Via Porto Vecchio 12*

WHERE TO STAY

CAMPING
Desenzano has two campsites: *Villagio Turistico Vo' (Via Vo' 4–9 | tel. 03 09 12 13 25 | www.voit.it)* and Camping San Francesco (Strada Vicinale San Francesco | tel. 03 09 11 02 45 | www.campingsanfrancesco.com).* Numerous other sites can be found in Valtenesi between Desenzano and Salò. Further information available from the tourist office in *San Felice del Benaco (Piazza Municipio 1 | tel. 0 36 56 25 41).*

HOTEL MAYER & SPLENDID
The erstwhile noble hotel is situated right on the promenade (unfortunately a busy through road). The plaster may be cracking on the ceiling but where else, at such a price, can you wake up and see the glittering water through French windows or breakfast on the balcony with a lakeside view? *57 rooms | Piazza Ulisse Papa 10 | tel. 03 09 14 22 53 | www.hotelmayerdesenzano.it | Moderate*

HOTEL NAZIONALE
This hotel was once one of the oldest in Desenzano; now it is the most modern. A cool, restrained, no-frills design. *41 rooms | Via Marconi 23 | tel. 03 09 15 85 55 | www.nazionaleonline.it | Moderate–Expensive*

PIROSCAFO

This small hotel has been in the Segattini family since the 1920s. Located right next to the old harbour in the heart of the Old Town. *32 rooms | Via Porto Vecchio 11 | tel. 03 09 14 11 28 | www.hotelpiroscafo.it | Moderate*

INSIDERTIP AZIENDA AGRICOLA PRATELLO ♺

Is everything organic here? Yes, even the pool is eco-certified in this *agriturismo* with hotel, restaurant and farm shop in a restored medieval hamlet. *16 rooms and 3 apartments | Via Pratello 26 | Padenghe sul Garda | tel. 03 09 90 70 05 | www.pratello.com | Moderate–Expensive*

INFORMATION

Via Porto Vecchio 34 | tel. 03 03 74 87 26 | www.gardalombardia.com

WHERE TO GO

SOLFERINO AND SAN MARTINO DELLA BATTAGLIA (141 E6) (*ℳ G8*)

The area around Lake Garda was frequently the scene of fierce battles. Among the bloodiest were the Battle of San Martino della Battaglia and the Battle of Solferino a few miles to the south. In 1859, the Italian Risorgimento, fighting for the unification of Italy, defeated the Austrian army under Emperor Franz Joseph. The foundations for a united Italy were laid. The unification of Italy included the Venetian Republic annexed from Austria, Piedmont ruled by the House of Savoy, the Kingdom of Sicily and papal Rome – and could only be achieved at the cost of 25,000 lives. And there were tens of thousands of wounded left on the battlefields to their own fate. This made the name Solferino known throughout the world. Henri Dunant, an extreme-ly rich Swiss man, was so shocked at the sight of these helpless soldiers that he founded the Red Cross – originally a charitable organisation set up to aid the wounded.

7000 skulls have been preserved in the church of *San Pietro* in Solferino as a reminder of the atrocities of war. *San Martino* also has a tower, the *Torre di San Mar-*

Looks pretty harmless today: a cannon in Solferino museum

tino, erected as a monument, 74 m/242.8 ft high. Inside, a series of frescoes relates to the history of the Risorgimento. *www.solferinoesanmartino.it*

SIRMIONE

▓ **MAP INSIDE BACK COVER**
(141 E4) (*ℳ G7*) **The town (pop. 8000) has a stunning location: the**

prominent peninsula juts out right in the middle of the south shore and points northwards.

Sirmione is one of the best-known towns on Lake Garda – it's hardly surprising that the pretty streets in the Old Town often get hopelessly crowded. The historical centre beyond the footbridge near the Scaliger castle can be visited only on foot – and due to the wide canal dug around the castle, the Old Town was turned into an island.

Sirmione has not just attracted tourists in modern times. In Roman days its thermal spa was well known. The hot sulphurous spring water, at almost 70°C/158°F, emerges from below the bed of the lake, 300 m/384 ft north-east of the 4 km-/2.5-long peninsula.

The Grotte di Catullo is an ancient Roman villa on the shores of the lake

SIGHTSEEING

GROTTE DI CATULLO ★

Catullus was right: he could hardly have chosen a more beautiful spot on Lake Garda. However, the representative villa, known as the Grotte di Catullo, was definitely not built by him as he was not wealthy enough.

But what does it matter whether the Roman poet Catullus ever lived on this spot at the south of the lake. It is a delightful location where he probably wrote his eulogy: "O beautiful Sirmione, the gem of all peninsulas and islands." An excursion to this impressive site is more than worthwhile: you can take a walk through olive groves and look at the extensive remains of the walls. The entrance fee includes a visit to the INSIDER TIP *archeological museum (Tue–Sat 8.30am–7.30pm (in winter until 5.30pm), Sun 9.30am–6.30pm (in winter until 2pm | www.grotte dicatullo.beniculturali.it)*. The clearly labelled displays provide a good overview of the whole site as well as of the early history of Lake Garda.

PARCO TOMELLERI ☀

Those who have had enough of the enoteca, ice cream shops and boutiques in the Old Town can enjoy the wonderful panoramic view of the lake in this park shaded by olive trees. This beautiful location is also a popular wedding venue *(www.sirmionewedding.it). Via Caio Valerio Catullo 7*

ROCCA SCALIGERA ★ ●

In the 13th century, Mastino della Scala had a moated castle built inside the protective walls on top of the Roman foundations. Occasionally exhibitions are held in the old fortress grounds at the entrance to the Old Town. But even without any cultural extras the castle has a lot on

The last car park outside the old town walls – cars are not permitted in the centre of Sirmione

offer, such as its  *tower* from where there is a lovely view over the rooftops of the Old Town.

St Anna's, with its 17th-century Baroque interior, is a little 14th-century church in the castle boasting 15th-century frescos. If you fancy some refreshments: for years now, a wonderful old fruit stand has been in place outside the castle, selling pieces of melon and quartered pine-apples, slices of lemon and coconut boats. *April–Oct Tue–Sat 8.30am–7.30pm, Sun 8.30am–1.30pm | www.polomuseale. lombardia.beniculturali.it*

FOOD & DRINK

LIDO DELLE BIONDE
This restaurant, which is only open in summer, sits at a wonderful location at the tip of the peninsula right on the lake. The pizza is delicious, the portions are large and the service is friendly. The *tag-lioni* with lake trout are a real treat! *Daily in the summer | Viale Carlo Gennari 28 |* *tel. 03 09 16 64 95 | www.lidodellebionde. it | Budget–Moderate*

LA RUCOLA
A feast for the eyes and taste buds (but expect prices to match): the romantical-ly lit Rucola will instantly attract you, just like the Michelin star menu with its inter-mediate courses and pralines. Be pre-pared for the impressive prices … *Closed Thu | Vicolo Strentelle 3 | tel. 03 0 91 63 26 | www.ristorantelarucola.it | Expensive*

LA SPERANZINA
Spicy spaghetti with *peperoncino* and red tuna tatare are among the speciali-ties of this antica trattoria. You can en-joy your meal in the peaceful garden with a view of the lake. *April–Oct daily | Via Dante 16 | tel. 03 09 90 62 92 | www. lasperanzina.it | Expensive*

OSTERIA AL TORCOL
This is a wine tavern with a minimal,

Dream away the time in Sirmione in the sun lounger and watch the sunset: a perfect holiday

but authentic menu. The osteria has friendly service and an extensive selection of wines mainly from regional producers. *Closed Wed | Via San Salvatore 30 | tel. 03 09 90 46 05 | Moderate–Expensive*

SHOPPING

The narrow streets of the Old Town on the peninsula are bursting with a huge variety of shops. The sulfurous thermal waters of Sirmione are said to help alleviate all kinds of illnesses, including ear, nose and throat issues. It's no wonder that all the pharmacies sell small nose sprays with INSIDER TIP "Acqua di Sirmione". Give one a try – it really does help!

MARKET

There is no weekly market in the Old Town, but one in *Colombare (Mon)* and in *Lugana di Sirmione (Fri)*.

LEISURE, SPORTS & BEACHES

Several free pebbly beaches are located on the south shore towards Peschiera. *Spiaggia Grotte di Catullo* is a treeless beach, free of charge, below the excavation site. Unfortunately it can be reached only by paddle boat or yacht. The ⭐ *Lido delle Bionde* is a large flat pebbly beach at the north-east end of the peninsula. There is a café and paddle-boat hire, sunbeds and umbrellas rather like at a classic Mediterranean resort, complete with a long wooden jetty which doubles as a sunbathing deck and catwalk. You can only access INSIDER TIP *Giamaica Beach* on foot. The beach at the end of the peninsula at the foot of the ruins lives up to its name: a flat shelf that drops into turquoise-blue water, a fabulous view and in some places even hot springs. Be careful: the flat stones can also be slippery!

The best place to enjoy the healing springs of Sirmione is *Aquaria (mid-April–Oct, main opening hours daily noon–10pm | Piazza Don A. Piatti 1 | www.terme-disirmione.com)*, the vast wellness centre of the thermal baths in Sirmione has several pools, rain-showers and all the accessories required for pure relaxation.

WHERE TO STAY

THE GARDA VILLAGE

A comfortable and attractive campsite located in Colombare on the lake with its own private beach. *Via Coorti Romane 47 | tel. 03 09 90 45 52 | www.gardavillage.it*

HOTEL MEUBLÉ GRIFONE

All rooms have a beautiful view of the lake despite being a small hotel in the narrow streets of the historical Old Town – and it is surprisingly cheap, too. *16 rooms | Via Gaetano Bocchio 4 | tel. 0 30 91 60 14 | www.gardaseegrifonehotel.eu | Moderate*

DEGLI OLEANDRI

Just the lobby tells you that this hotel is family run. Oil paintings hang on the walls of the staircase and carefully chosen antiques give the place an atmosphere of its own. *24 rooms | Via Dante Alighieri 31 | tel. 03 09 90 57 80 | www.hoteldeglioleandri.it | Moderate*

PACE

From the hotel windows there is a wonderful view over the lake. *22 rooms | Piazza Porto Valentino 5 | tel. 03 09 90 58 77 | www.pacesirmione.it | Moderate*

CAMPING SIRMIONE

This three-star campsite with its own beach is closest to the Old Town. *Colombare | Via Sirmioncino 9 | tel. 030 91 90 45 | www.camping-sirmione.it*

VILLA CORTINE PALACE HOTEL

You'll feel like you've been transported back to the 19th century in one of the prettiest hotels in town. Lovely park. *55 rooms | Viale Gennari 2 | tel. 03 09 90 58 90 | www.palacehotelvillacortine.it | Expensive*

VILLA PIOPPI

An old villa on the lake, a 15 minute walk from the Old Town. Very basic but charming and in a beautiful location. 7 rooms | *Via XXV Aprile 76 | tel. 03 09 90 41 19 | www.villapioppihotel.com | Moderate*

INFORMATION

Viale Marconi 8 | tel. 03 03 74 87 21 | iat.sirmione@provincia.brescia.it

LOW BUDGET

Places for lunch can by found outside the Old Towns of Sirmione and Desenzano, especially on main roads, offering a low priced *pranzo al lavoro* – usually a three-course meal for 10 euros. Plain, Italian and filling – a "meal for workers".

Even though the end-of-season sales in Italy are no longer the institution that they once were, bargain hunters can reckon with discounts of up to 50 percent in July and August. The outlet centres are also worth a try because the already reduced prices drop a bit more during the *saldi*: e.g. *Fashion District Mantova (www.mantovaoutlet.it)* on the A 22, exit Mantova Sud.

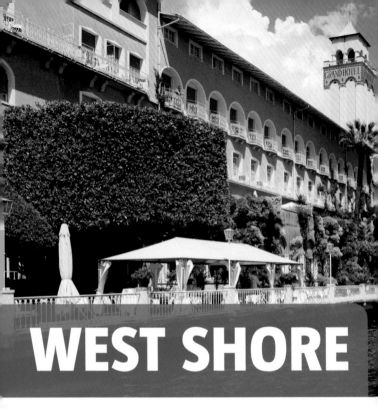

WEST SHORE

And how did it all begin? In 1880 the German Louis Wimmer travelled down the west side of the lake and recognised how much his fellow countrymen would like it. He began by building the Grand Hotel Gardone and, as such, set the stone rolling for tourism on Lake Garda. In the early 20th century, ever more luxury hotels went up, and instead of lemon trees, vineyards and olive groves, beautiful parks were laid out, whose old trees from those days still give this region its special charm. In 1921 the Italian poet Gabriele D'Annunzio, an eccentric and a dandy, came to live here. His house, Vittoriale degli Italiani, is now a museum and still retains the spirit of that time. That spirit, however, was soon to turn into a phantom – in 1943 Benito Mussolini declared the Facist *Repubblica Sociale Italiana* while in neighbouring Salò. Mussolino was living with his family at the Villa Feltrinelli in Gargnano, and he had arranged for his lover, Claretta Petacci, to stay in the Villa Fiordaliso, also in Gardone, which today is a first-class restaurant. At the southern end of the west shore the mountains have taken a step back from the lake. There are no more tunnels here and the lakeside road winds its way elegantly along the shore-line or turns inland so that the old fishing villages huddled around their harbours, that form the commune of Gargnano, remain undisturbed. Whoever comes here on holiday is not looking for an extreme sports adventure as in the north, nor for the family-friendly beaches along the east shore. Instead, visitors are more likely to be looking for a good cappuccino

The quieter corner of the lake favoured by the Italians: luxury living and gourmet dining on the west shore

next to the lake – which at this point is so wide it can seem like the open sea when the weather is hazy. In the evening, the holiday-maker here likes to go out to eat, for this is where the best dining can be had.

GARDONE RIVIERA

(141 D–E2) *(ﾉ F–G 5–6)* **Even in the high season, the cafés here are never** **overflowing. A table can always be found after a gentle stroll along the Lungolago – this is where the more leisurely tastes are well catered for.**

The best thing about Gardone are its parks and gardens. Taking the steep roads and paths that lead up from the shore, you will find yourself walking in the shade of old cypress trees and magnolias. The gardens, along with the stately villas and old hotels, are testimony to Gardone's glorious past. A stay in Lungolago D'Annunzio can work wonders: here

The Vittoriale: a bizarre cabinet of curiosities, former home of the poet D'Annunzio

GIARDINO BOTANICO ANDRÉ HELLER ★ ●

Originally this botanic garden was just one of the many wonderful parks in the village, but since the Austrian artist and performer André Heller bought it at the end of the 1980s, it has become more than just that. Clanging fountains can be found among huge trees, and in one or other secret corner a modern sculpture by Keith Haring or Mimmo Paladino. André Heller enthuses about his collection of flora from different places from around the world, a paradise that he never ceases to wonder at: "Edelweiss in the middle of orchid meadows, ferns several feet high next to magnificent pomegranates. Streams and waterfalls with sacred koi, trout and reflections made by dragonflies, hills of dolomite rock next to cactii and towering ivies." *Daily March–Oct 9am–7pm | www.hellergarden.com*

MUSEO IL DIVINO INFANTE

The world's first (and supposedly only) museum of the Christ Child: the 200 sculptures that make up this collection date from a period of three centuries and are truly unique. *Easter–Sept Fri–Sun 3pm–7pm, mid-Dec–mid-Jan Tue–Sun 2pm–6pm (Dec 20–Jan 6 daily 10am–6pm) | Via dei Colli 34 | www.il-bambino-gesu.com*

VITTORIALE DEGLI ITALIANI ★

Are you fascinated by the life of one of the most enigmatic personalities of Italian history? Then visit the "victory monument of the Italians". The war hero, philosopher, poet, Fascist and maverick, Gabriele D'Annunzio (1863–1938), not only built a house here in 1921, but also an almost inaccessible and bizarre collection of buildings. The attractions, which

you can easily forget that the village is not even on the lakeside but above it. Gardone Sopra, with its houses all huddled around San Nicola's parish church, now has a population of 2700. A ❄ INSIDER TIP narrow path with a magnificent view of the lake winds its way between the houses. And everyone heads for *the* attraction *par excellence*, Vittoriale degli Italiani, the poet Gabriele D'Annunzio's retirement home.

are worth seeing in addition to the poet's house, include a war museum with the legendary plane from which D'Annunzio dropped leaflets over Vienna during World War One, a warship, the mausoleum as well as Isotta Fraschini vintage car and old Fiat T4. In the open-air theatre, cultural events are regularly performed during the summer *(www.anfiteatrodelvit toriale.it)*. In *Vittoriale park* visitors are free to roam, whereas guided tours are obligatory in the *house*. As admission tickets are limited, it is best to purchase them beforehand online. *Daily 9am–5pm, April–Oct until 8pm, museum and house Nov–March Closed Mon | www.vittoriale.it*

FOOD & DRINK

AGLI ANGELI

Patrizia and Elisabetta Pellegrini's cooking in Gardone Sopra is becoming more and more elegant and refined. Reservations essential! *Closed Tue | Via Dosso 7 | tel. 0 36 52 09 91 | www.agliangeli.biz | Moderate–Expensive*

ANTICO BROLO

Delectable and creative traditional fare is served right in the town centre. The chefs Enrico and Marcello are very attentive and do their best to ensure for a pleasant dining experience. *Closed Mon | Via Carere 10 | tel. 0 36 52 14 21 | www.ristorante anticobrolo.it | Moderate–Expensive*

LIDO 84 ☆

The view of the lake doesn't get more spectacular – and the food lives up to expectations: the restaurant has a Michelin star and offers the surprising combination of typical ingredients from the Lombardy region with exotic spices. *Closed Wed lunchtime and Tue | Corso Zanardelli 196 | tel. 0 36 52 00 19 | www.ristorante lido84.com | Expenisve*

TRATTORIA RIOLET

Whether you order the home-made antipasti, one of the many pasta dishes or hearty grilled meat, the traditional fair in this typical trattoria has a new twist. The wonderful view from the ☆ terrace

---

MARCO POLO HIGHLIGHTS

makes up for the many steps you have to climb to get to this jewel of a restaurant. Make sure to reserve a table! *Closed Wed| Via Fasano di Sopra 75 | located in Fasano | tel. 0 36 52 05 45 | Budget–Moderate*

SHOPPING

VINTAGE MARKET

A small flea market is held along the promenade once a month where you can find antiques and objects from the sixties and seventies. The dates vary.

LEISURE, SPORTS & BEACHES

Spiaggia Rimbalzello to the south of the town costs 5 euros (11 euros incl. umbrella and sun-bed). Free beaches are near the Villa delle Rose in Fasano and another, very small one can be found near the casino on Via Zanardelli. At *Big Sur Sky Park (Via Val di Sur | tel. 34 72 28 43 61 | www.rimbalzelloadven ture. com)* in San Michele, those who dare can undertake a tandem paragliding adventure.

ENTERTAINMENT

Gardone is better known for its culture than its nightlife. Live music can be enjoyed free of charge along the lake promenade on alternate evenings; in Vittoriale there are theatre performances and concerts *(www.anfiteatrodelvittoriale.it)*. One of the more stylish places to go on the lake is the former lighthouse **INSIDER TIP** *Torre San Marco (Tue–Sun 10.30pm–3am | Via Zanardelli 132 | www.torresanmarco. it)* with its piano bar and club. *Caffè Wimmer (Piazza Wimmer 5)* or *Bar Le Rose (Via dei Caduti 19)* in Gardone Sopra are also nice.

WHERE TO STAY

HOTEL DIANA

The hotel's rooms are plain, but with balconies and a view of the lake – at a good price. *18 rooms | Lungolago Gabriele D'Annunzio 30 | tel. 0 36 52 18 15 | www.hoteldianagardone.it | Budget–Moderate*

DUE DI MORO

Neat, fresh and high quality – you can expect this from the country holiday with Luca and his family. Meticulous attention is paid to harmony with nature. The food is strictly vegetarian, or vegan on request, and the rooms are spacious and deliberately have no television. The restaurant is open to non-residents on weekends. *5 rooms | Via Ceriolo 23–25 | tel. 0 36 52 01 01 | www.duedimoro.com | Moderate*

INSIDER TIP PREMIGNAGA COUNTRY HOUSE & RESORT

Whether for a honeymoon or just a weekend getaway, a stay in the picturesque surroundings of this former monastery high above Gardone is unforgettable. Daniela Ondelli welcomes her guests warmly and pampers them with many small details. *10 flats | Morgnaga di Gardone Riviera | Via della Chiesa 47 | tel. 0 36 52 21 15 | www.premignaga.it | Expensive*

SAVOY PALACE

This beautiful grand hotel can look back at a 100-year-old history and many famous guests. Half of the complex is given over to flats, but part of it is still a hotel. The standard is high, the view fantastic, as is the small pool. *60 rooms | Corso Zanardelli 2 | tel. 03 65 29 05 88 | www.savoypalacegar dasee.com | Expensive*

LE TRE GATTE

B&B in a quiet street. The owner's mother was English; the furnishings have something of a British country house about them. *4 rooms | Vicolo Ars 10 | tel. 03 65 29 04 40 | www.letregatte.com | Budget*

INFORMATION

Corso Repubblica 1 | tel. 0 36 52 06 36 | iat.gardoneriviera@provincia.brescia.it

(Closed Mon in winter | Via Panoramica 96 | tel. 0 36 52 09 05 | Budget). Make a reservation on Sundays!

TOSCOLANO-MADERNO
(141 E2) (*ⅅ G5*)

The twin community (pop. 8000) lies slightly to the north, where the Toscolano feeds into the lake. Its upper course is the *Valle delle Cartiere*, the "paper factory valley", which is well worth a visit. Back in the 14th century, the paper mills

Maritime still life: moored boats along the promenade in Maderno

WHERE TO GO

SAN MICHELE ☆ (141 D2) (*ⅅ F5*)

If you like, you can take the hour-long walk up to the village of San Michele. The path (waymarked from Vittoriale) misses out all the twists and turns of the road. At the top, hearty traditional dishes and delicious tiramisu wait at *Miramonti*

were already selling their wares throughout Europe, and later even in the Orient. A path passes by the ruins. It's best to start from the Gardesana by the turn to Gaino. Two millstones on the path can be seen. These were used to turn rags into pulp for the production of paper. After about 30 mins you will reach the very well presented *Museo della Carta*

(April–Sept daily 10am–6pm, Sat/Sun 10am–5pm | www.valledellecartiere.it).

⭐ Sant'Andrea Apostolo church in Maderno is worth seeing even if you don't notice it at first as the more recent parish church opposite dominates the scene. The 12th-century Romanesque chapel with its façade of pink, grey and white stripes is more worthwhile. Look for the

The *Osteria del Boccondivino (closed lunchtimes and on Tue | Via Cavour 71 | tel. 03 65 64 25 12 | Moderate)* in Maderno specialises in fish. The ⓥ *Ristorante San Marco (daily | Piazza San Marco 5 | tel. 03 65 64 11 03 | www.hsmarco.it | Expensive)*, also located in Maderno, is an exclusive restaurant not far from the lake that has adopted the ideals of the

Cast a glance into the Baroque garden in the Villa Bettoni-Cazzago when driving past

details in the porch (fruit, leaf tendrils, plaited ornamentation): the skill of the masons almost a millenium ago is amazing. The harmonious interior is dominated by heavy pillars and columns with their imposing capitals. Yet a millenium older even is the Roman INSIDER TIP ▶ *Villa Nonii Arrii* in Toscolano *(April–Oct Sat/Sun 10am–noon and 3pm–6pm | Piazza Santissima Maria del Benaco)* with its well-preserved mosaic pavements.

"slow-food" fraternity, producing regional dishes. The tastefully renovated 🎗 *Hotel Milano (Lungolago Zanardelli 12 | tel. 03 65 54 05 95 | www.hotelmilano maderno.com | Moderate–Expensive)* is set far enough back from the through-road and has a beautiful view of the lake – and its own pool. The *Hotel Vienna* in the Old Town does not have a view of the lake *(17 rooms | Via Giuseppe Garibaldi 43 | tel. 03 65 64 10 83 | Budget)*.

Information: V*ia Garibaldi 24 | tel. 03 65 64 10 83 | www.provincia.brescia.it/ turismo* and *Via Ugo Foscolo 3 | tel. 03 03 74 87 41*

GARGNANO

(141 F1) *(Ø G5)* **Once you have had enough of all the tunnels on the west shore (if you come from the north) and can breathe out again having just passed through the last one, you will reach Gargnano (pop. 3000).**

The name actually applies to three little villages, each with a harbour, the first as lovely as the last. First of all you will come to the largest of the three, Gargnano itself, with its short lakeside promenade, followed by Villa and then Bogliaco, skirted by the Gardesana road and each with just one one-way road leading into the village. Before the Gardesana was built in the 1930s, the most common way of getting about was by boat.

Hiking and strolling, swimming and dining – these are the reasons for coming here. And in the evening the same slow pace doesn't change. Gargnano got out of step once for a short time: during the Fascist period of the "Republic of Salò" near the end of World War Two, the dictator Benito Mussolini had his official residence here in the Villa Feltrinelli.

SIGHTSEEING

MARINA DI BOGLIACO

The harbour in Bogliaco is elegant and exclusive and surrounded by only a few houses in this small community. You can admire the sleek yachts and smart sailing boats – especially in September when the biggest sailing regatta on Lake Garda is held here and several hundred participants and sailing enthusiasts gather.

PALAZZO FELTRINELLI

The palazzo was requisitioned by the Fascist government in the 1940s and was used as the general headquarters of Benito Mussolini. Today, the University of Milan holds a summer school here with INSIDER TIP Italian language courses *(www.unimi.it)* for students from around the world. *Via Castello 4*

VILLA BETTONI-CAZZAGO

A magnificent building! The special thing about the privately owned villa in the district of Bogliaco is the architectural consistency that harmoniously defines the villa as well as its perfectly landscaped garden that is usually open in April for a garden show.

FOOD & DRINK

RISTORANTE FORNICO

Are you looking for a rustic dining experience? Every Sunday Marco grills meat kebabs and serves them with polenta – a popular dish with the locals. Otherwise, the cuisine is traditional and delicious. *Closed Mon and Tue evenings | Via Sole 13 | tel. 0 36 57 10 58 | www.ris torantefornico.it | Budget–Moderate*

RISTORANTE AL MIRALAGO 🌿

Here you can sit under an awning, protected from the sun, and look out across the lake. A modest menu with typical regional dishes and plenty of fish, along with matching wines. *Closed Tue | Lungolago Zanardelli 5 | tel. 0 36 57 12 09 | Moderate*

OSTERIA DEL RESTAURO

The pace of everyday life at Villa harbour is gentle. If this is to your taste then the osteria is just right for you. The home-made tortellini, the spicy bacon (lardo) and the antipasti are all delicious.

Closed Wed | Piazza Villa 19 | tel. 0 36 57 26 43 | Moderate

TRATTORIA SAN MARTINO

A simple, traditional and fantastically Italian restaurant. The chef loves to prepare surprise dishes that are not on the menu. The terrace is also quite romantic. Make a reservation! *Closed Mon | Via Roma 33 | tel. 0 36 57 14 36 | www.trattoriasanmartino.it | Moderate*

ALLO SCOGLIO

Here you can eat in a pretty garden in Bogliaco on the lakeside. The building is a former gatehouse to the Villa Bettoni-Cazzago. Fish is a speciality here. *Closed Mon | Via Barbacane 2 | tel. 0 36 57 10 30 | www.alloscoglio.it | Moderate*

LEISURE, SPORTS & BEACHES

The ⭐ *Parco Fontanella*, to the north of the villages, is free of charge and has a beach. Here you can lie in the shade of the olive trees; there is table tennis and techno music, a big car park (parking fee) and the *OK-Surf* surfing school *(tel. 32 84 71 77 77 | www.oksurf.it)*.

ENTERTAINMENT

The pace in Gargnano is leisurely – which is precisely why regular visitors love this resort. After dinner, you can treat yourself to an ice cream on the lakeside. The biggest and best are served in the *Bar Azzurra (Piazza Angelo Feltrinelli 11)*.

WHERE TO STAY

ANTICA CASCINA LIANO ● �

The perfect retreat: in Liano, 600 m/ 1969 ft up, this fully renovated building with heavy wooden ceilings and rustic interior is situated in farming country. This former farmhouse has extensive views of the lake. *6 flats | Via Liano 1 | tel. 0 36 57 28 70 | www.anticacascinaliano.it | Moderate*

HOTEL DU LAC

This hotel, situated directly on the lake in Villa, is now in the third generation of the Arosio family. The antique furnishings in most rooms are lovely. *11 rooms | Via Colletta 21 | tel. 0 36 57 11 07 | www.hoteldulac.it | Moderate–Expensive*

LEFAY RESORT & SPA ● � ◉

Magnificent 5-star complex high above the lake, ultra-modern, with floorboards of olive wood and a large pool, a huge spa facility extending over ¾ acres, and a top-class restaurant. When it was built, considerable thought was given to its ecological impact with the use of energy-saving technology. *90 rooms | Via Angelo Feltrinelli 118 | tel. 03 65 24 18 00 | www.lefayresorts.com | Expensive*

HOTEL MEANDRO �

At first glance this modest-looking hotel may not appeal immediately, but the view will make up for that. All rooms (incl. the restaurant) in this family-run hotel have panoramic views of the lake. There is a swimming-pool with a roof and the large public beach is close-by. A ceramic artist *(www.marianofuga.it)* from Vicenza exhibits charming figurines in the building next door. *44 rooms | Via Repubblica 44 | tel. 0 36 57 11 28 | www.hotelmeandrogardasee.com | Moderate–Expensive*

INFORMATION

Piazzale Boldini 2 | tel. 03 65 79 12 43 | www.gargnanosulgarda.it

WHERE TO GO

LAGO D'IDRO AND
LAGO DI VALVESTINO
(136 B–C 5–6) (*F–G 3–4*)

A curvy little road leads from Gargnano through the surprisingly untouched countryside that has yet to see much tourist traffic to INSIDER TIP *Lago di Valvestino*. With its crystal clear water, this reser-

Cima Rest (sign up at the Consorzio Forestale Terra tra i due Laghi | tel. 03 65 74 50 07 | www.osservatoriocimarest.it) located at the tip of the lake on the Cima Rest plateau. The website of the forestry association (*www.consorzioforestalevalvestino.com*) provides more interesting information about Valvestino.

A serpentine road runs steeply back down to the shimmering water of *Lake*

Let's go lake-hopping: Lago di Valvestino and Lago d'Idro further inland form Gargnano

voir has a wild kind of beauty. The Toscolano stream, which powers the paper mills in Toscolano-Maderno, is dammed by the lake. Take a look at the old barns at *Borgo Cima Rest (4 apartments for 6 people | located in Cima Rest | tel. 0 36 57 40 67 | www.lavalvestino.com/borgocimarest | Budget)* where nature-lovers can spend the night. On select dates from May to September, you can visit the INSIDER TIP *Osservatorio Astronomico di*

Idro. The whole region has a certain mountainous Tyrolean feel but the villages are Italian with their narrow streets and Romanesque churches. In *Pieve Vecchia*, at the south end of the lake, you can stop for a break in one of the street cafés and watch the motorbikes pass or head for the *Pizzeria Milano (Closed Tue | Via Trento 35 | tel.03 65 82 33 91 | www.hotelmilano.bs.it | Budget)* for a bite to eat, which has a modest hotel attached. Information: *Via Trento 27 | Idro | tel. 0 36 58 32 24 | www.lagodidro.it*

MADONNA DI MONTECASTELLO ☼
(137 E6) *(⚲ H4)*

This hermitage, at an altitude of 700 m/2297 ft just a few miles to the north, is a popular place for day-trippers and pilgrims alike (see p. 109), with a

harbour – are nestled between the steep rock canyons and lush meadows of the Alto Garda Bresciano National Park high above the lake. With their historic roots, folksy character and culinary traditions, these villages have a particular kind of charm. Local specialities such as cheese, salami and sausages can be purchased from the *agriturismo* ● *Alpe del Garda*

Do you have vertigo? Villages in the community of Tremosine are high above the west shore

wonderful view of Lake Garda and the mountains. *Daily Easter–Oct 9am–6pm | www.santuariomontecastello.it*

TREMOSINE (137 E5) *(⚲ H3–4)*

Aromatic alpine cheese, untouched nature and amazing views make the quiet plateau in the municipality of Tremosine a paradise for connoisseurs, nature-lovers and sports fans. All of the eighteen villages – apart from Campione with its

(Daily | Via Provinciale 1 | located in Polzone | tel. 03 65 95 30 50 | www.alpedelgarda.it | Budget) with its show cheese dairy, farm shop and playground.

The main centre, *Pieve*, is just less than 20 km/12.4 mi north of Gargnano, high above the lake. Visitors are attracted by the ★ ● terrazza del brivido – and this is what the *Hotel Paradiso (22 rooms | tel. 03 65 95 30 12 | www.terrazzadelbrivido.it | Moderate)* advertises with: its terrace really does jut out frighteningly far over the lake below. Near the terrace of hotel *Miralago (29 rooms | tel. 03 65 95 30 01 | www.miralago.it | Budget)*, there is a narrow path that takes you down the seemingly vertical cliff face. This path, the INSIDERTIP *Sentiero del Porto*, is marked as route 201 and was once the only way down to the lake. Today, the breathtaking *Strada della Forra* (see p. 107) road, which was built in 1913 through the narrow gorge of the Brasa torrrent, also takes you to the town. For the very active, sample what is on offer at Thomas Engels' INSIDERTIP *Skyclimber (Via Dalco 3 | tel. 3 35 29 32 37 | www.sky climber.it)*: this includes canyoning trips, mountain-bike training circuit and guided roped-climbing tours. There are also many possibilities for children. *Information in Pieve: Piazza Marconi | tel. 03 65 95 31 85 | www.infotremosine.org*

SALÒ

MAP INSIDE BACK COVER
(141 D2) (ΩΩ F6) **Salò (pop. 11,000)** has had the longest ★ promenade on **Lake Garda for more than 100 years – it was built after an earthquake in 1901.**
In 2004 there was another earthquake which badly damaged a number of buildings. However, the lakeside promenade has since been widened and extended. It now runs for almost 3 km/1.9 mi right round to the cemetery on the other side of the bay with its eye-catching cypresses. It is virtually car-free, with one café after another, and benches lining the shore. The little fishing boats bobbing about in the water are taken out into the lake in the mornings in search of what the gourmet restaurants in Salò later serve their guests: lavarello and corregone – Lake Garda whitefish. The town nestles in a bay at the southern end of the west shore and, even if today it is a busy little place, the former spa town still exudes a certain elegance.

Salò has always been wealthier than the neighbouring fishing villages. In 1377 it was declared the administrative centre for the west shore by the ruling Visconti of Milan. And in 1426 the Venetians named Salò the "Magnifica Patria della Riviera". Towards the end of the more recent period under Fascist rule, Mussolini raised Salò to the capital of the Fascist Socialist Republic.

SIGHTSEEING

HOTEL LAURIN
The Laurin is the most beautiful Art Deco building on the Lake. It is now an elegant hotel. If you only want a drink you can go into the lobby and marvel at the exquisite interior at your leisure. During the Fascist dictatorship, the building housed the Foreign Ministry for a time as well as the dictator Benito Mussolini himself. *Viale Landi 9 | www.hotel laurinsalo.com*

PALAZZO DEL PODESTÀ
In the 16th century the old Town Hall from the 14th century was given a Vene-

LOW BUDGET

200 shops offering reductions of up to 70 % on brand products: in Rodengo Saiano in the *Franciacorta Outlet Village (Tue–Sun 10am–8pm, Mon 2.30pm–8pm, in summer Sat/Sun until 9pm | 6 km/3.7 mi beyond Brescia, exit: Ospitaletto | www.francia cortaoutlet.it).*

tian façade with an arcade, and it suits the building very well. However nothing of the original remains – the earthquake in 1901 also destroyed the Palazzo del Podestà.

Making you melt: at the Vassalli the motto is "give a little kiss"!

SANTA MARIA ANNUNZIATA

Salò is the only place on Lake Garda with a cathedral. Work started on the late Gothic building in 1453. A white Renaissance portal was later added to the plain brick façade. *Daily 8am–noon and 3pm–7pm | Piazza Duomo | www.parrocchiadisalo.it*

FOOD & DRINK

LA CAMPAGNOLA 🏵

Angelo Dal Bon's restaurant is one of the best in the area; the cuisine is according to the "slow food" principle. The food leaves as little to be desired as the unbeatable extensive wine list. A gourmet speciality is the INSIDER TIP salt-coated Entrecote rib steak. Reservation essential! *Closed Tue lunchtime and all day Mon | Via Brunati 11 | tel. 0 36 52 21 53 | www.lacampagnola1952.com | Expensive*

LA CASA DEL DOLCE

This is where you'll find probably the creamiest chocolate ice cream anywhere on the lake. You can watch it being made in the parlour next door. *Piazza Duomo 1*

LOLLIPOP

This *yoghurteria* has the fruitiest ice cream in town, as lots of yoghurt is used. Twice as refreshing in summer! *Lungolago Zanardelli 43*

INSIDER TIP POLENTERIA

Polenta – are you also a fan of this rustic comfort food? Then sample the unusual creations at the Leali brothers who conjure up all kinds of dishes with the North Italians' favourite side dish. You will be amazed and the friendly eatery 4 km/2.5 mi south in *Cunettone di Salò* will become a firm favourite! *Closed Sun evenings and Mon | Via Europa 9 | tel. 0 36 54 21 11 | Budgeting*

TRATTORIA ALLE ROSE

Gianni Briarava serves only the very best in his contemporary-style restaurant. The classic cucina gardesana has been blended with new recipes ranging from pasta with beans, grilled horse meat or more refined fish dishes. *Closed Wed | Via Gasparo da Salò 33 | tel. 0 36 54 32 20 | www. trattoriaallerose.it | Moderate–Expensive*

PASTICCERIA VASSALLI

Tasty sandwiches are on offer here, numerous cakes and *bacetti di Salò* – "kisses from Salò" – delicious nut praliné chocolates. *Closed Tue in winter | Via San Carlo 84–86 | www.pasticceria-vassalli.it*

SHOPPING

The Old Town in Salò is perfect for shopping as it has many more shops than in the smaller villages. Most are in *Via San Carlo*, that runs parallel to and slightly set back from the shore.

MARKET

Every Sat morning, south of the Old Town. This is one of the biggest markets on the lake.

MELCHIORETTI

This grocery shop looks like a chemist's – and that's exactly what it used to be. Built in 1805, it has remained virtually unchanged since 1870 – except that instead of soap bars you'll find pesto and pasta. *Piazza Zanelli 11*

VOM FASS

This shop is equivalent to a sweet shop for adults: liqueurs, olive oil, vinegar and chutney. All products are the finest quality ... superb! *Closed Sun/Mon | Piazza Sergio Bresciani 3*

LEISURE, SPORTS & BEACHES

When the promenade was extended two small beaches were created opposite the bay, not far from the cemetery. They are easy to pick out thanks to the distinctive row of cypresses. Close by is the *Valtenesi* – a hilly area around Manerba. Here, you will find a number of other places to swim: *Porto San Felice* has a flat pebbly beach; dogs are not allowed on the *Spiaggia La Romantica* in Manerba which also has a restaurant. In the evenings, there is live music on the free-of-charge beach at the *Baia Bianca (www.baiabian ca.it)*. You can wade on foot through the shallow water to the isle of *San Biagio,* popular with the younger generation. In *Moniga del Garda* there are pebbly and rocky beaches that are free of charge.

One of the most beautiful places to jog on Lake Garda is the route around the traffic-free bay of Salò. The best time is in the morning when relatively few people are out and about. There are also many cycle paths around Salò, including one that leads to Lonato near Desenzano. About 1 km/0.6 mi north-east of Salò in *Barbarano* is the *Rimbalzello Adventure Parco Avventura (June–Aug daily 10am–8pm, April/May and Sept/Oct Sat 2pm–7pm, Sun 10am–7pm | 19–24 euros | www.rim balzelloadventure.com)*. Here, those looking for adventure can climb swaying rope bridges and shaky tree trunks.

ENTERTAINMENT

The whole length of the Lungolago in Salò is given over to strolling in the evening. Just drift along, back and forth.

AL BARETTO

An inconspicuous bar on the lakeside promenade – but the proprietor, Gigi, has the best selection of open wines, such as Bellavista, a sparkling wine from Franciacorta. This is where local wine-lovers meet for an aperitif or for a midnight drink. *Lungolago Zanardelli 46*

Scramble through the ruins and admire the view: excursion to Rocca in Manerba

PLAZA DISCO

Things don't really get going in this disco in the western suburbs until around midnight. Hits and beats for all ages are played in the three different rooms. *Via Domenico Signori 41 | Roè Volciano | www.plazadisco.it*

WHERE TO STAY

AGRITURISMO IL BAGNOLO

Fancy a holiday on a farm just a few miles from Lake Garda? Located way above the lake and for those who love the peace and quiet, it's ideal. Milk is still fresh from the cow here, cold meat and cheese are all produced on the farm. *9 rooms | Bagnolo di Serniga | tel. 0 36 52 02 90 | www.ilbagnolo.it | Budget–Moderate*

BELLERIVE

This hotel at the marina has a pretty location on the promenade, a lovely garden and an even more beautiful view from the little ❄ balconies. *49 rooms | Via Pietro da Salò 11 | tel. 03 65 52 04 10 | www.hotelbellerive.it | Expensive*

BED & BREAKFAST AI COLLI ❄

This new building with a wonderful view of the lake is situated in a quiet residential area above the through-road. *5 rooms | Via Carla Mortari 6 | tel. 32 92 52 23 68 | www.bblagodigarda.it | Budget*

HOTEL DUOMO

This very friendly hotel is next to the cathedral on the long lakeside promenade. *24 rooms | Lungolago Zanardelli 63 | tel.*

0 36 52 10 26 | www.hotelduomosalo.it |
Expensive

HOTEL GAMBERO

This was one of the cheapest hotels in Salò for some time, then it became almost derelict. It has now been beautifully renovated and re-opened. Reserve one of the quieter rooms with a view of the lake. *25 rooms | Piazza Carmine 1 | tel. 03 65 29 09 41 | Moderate*

INFORMATION

Piazza Sant'Antonio 4 | tel. 0 36 52 14 23 | www.prolocosalo.it

WHERE TO GO

ISOLA DEL GARDA (141 E3) *(🛱 G6)*
Even if the only larger isle in the lake with the magnificent villa and the INSIDER TIP wonderfully manicured park is in private ownership, during the summer months it can be visited from various places on the lake as part of organized tours. Tours from Salò start on Sundays at 10am. *Booking necessary: tel. 32 86 12 69 43 | www.isoladelgarda.com*

MANERBA DEL GARDA
(141 D3) *(🛱 F6)*
This little town (pop. 5000) about 10 km/6.2 mi to the south is known for its picturesque shoreline with the small harbour of Porto Dusano and long beaches. From 🔻 *Rocca di Manerba*, the castle ruins atop a striking cliff near Montinelle, you can enjoy a wonderful view of the southern side of the lake. The ruins are part of the Rocca di Manerba Natural Archaeological Park. To make it easier for visitors to explore this area with its rich history, an innovative INSIDER TIP bike-sharing system, *Manerba in Bici*, has been set up – for more info: *Manerba*

Servizi Turistici (Via Zanardelli 17 | tel. 03 65 55 27 45 | www.manerbaservizituristici.eu).
In Manerba's hinterland, surrounded by olive trees, lies the INSIDER TIP *Azienda Agricola Manestrini (Soiano del Lago | Via Avanzi 11 | tel. 03 65 50 22 31 | www.manestrini.it)*. The complex consists of an oil mill, a fine restaurant with a view of the lake and holiday flats. Every Tuesday evening at 5.30pm, the oil mill invites you to an aperitif *(5 euros)*: After a guided tour, visitors can taste the olive oil and other native products. And if you reserve a table for dinner at the restaurant (*Moderate–Expensive*), you get the aperitif for free.

SAN FELICE DEL BENACO
(141 D3) *(🛱 F6)*
Most campsites on Lake Garda are to be found between Salò and Desenzano; hotels are noticeably fewer in number here. The beaches tend to be pretty full and, although access to most of the beaches not owned by the campsites is free of charge, the carparks are not. On top of that, many day-visitors come here at the weekends. But away from the lake you can wind your way between vineyards and olive groves. The centre of San Felice (pop. 3400) and its churches are worth a detour. There is a small beach near Porto Portese for swimming.
Homemade pasta and a massive serving of fish starters are available in Porto Portese at the *Ristorante Osvaldo (Daily | Piazzale Marinai d'Italia 5 | tel. 0 36 56 21 08 | Moderate)*. The *Park Hotel Casimiro Village* is a huge hotel with a matching swimming pool *(198 rooms | Via Porto Portese 22 | tel. 03 65 62 62 62 | www.parkhotelcasimiro.it | Moderate)*. Good olive oil can be found at *Frantoio Cooperativa Agricola San Felice del Benaco (Via delle Gere 2 | www.oliofelice.com)*.

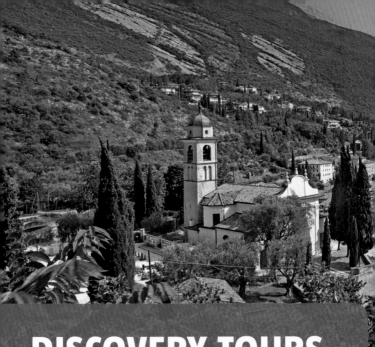

DISCOVERY TOURS

① LAKE GARDA AT A GLANCE

START: ① Riva	
END: ① Riva	**7 days**
Distance: approx. 170 km/106 mi	

COSTS: approx. 85 euros/person (bus and boat tickets, admission fees)

WHAT TO PACK: swimming kit, good walking shoes

IMPORTANT TIPS: the most important bus lines around the lake are as follows: Bus no. 183/184 Riva– Malcesine–Garda–Peschiera, Bus no. 26 Peschiera–Sirmione– Desenzano, Bus no. 27 Desenzano–Salò–Gardone–Limone–Riva. Schedules and prices can be found at *www.atv.verona.it*, *www.trasportibrescia.it* and *www.ttesercizio.it*; Lake Garda ferry timetables are available at *www.navigazionelaghi.it*.

Would you like to explore the places that are unique to this region? Then the Discovery Tours are just the thing for you – they include terrific tips for stops worth making, breathtaking places to visit, selected restaurants and fun activities. It's even easier with the Touring App: download the tour with map and route to your smartphone using the QR Code on pages 2/3 or from the website address in the footer below – and you'll never get lost again even when you're offline.

TOURING APP

→ p. 2/3

This route explores the highlights of the largest lake in all of Italy. The north side is a paradise for outdoor lovers and a mecca for surfers, while the southwest has a bit of a Belle Époque flair and the bathing beaches in the southeast are ideal for families. If you decide to take the bus from point to point rather than a car, you can also sit back and enjoy a few leisurely boat rides along the way.

On the northern shore, the lake still has a very alpine feel, and it sits like a fjord surrounded by mountains up to 2000 m/ 6562 ft high. All kinds of sports are on offer in ❶ **Riva** → p. 41 and ❷ **Torbole** → p. 45. You can go climbing,

DAY 1

❶ Riba
3 km/1.9 mi

❷ Torbole
14 km/8.7 mi

An abundance of flowers and nostalgic villas awaits up and down the steps of Gardone Riviera

❸ Malcesine

DAY 2

32 km/19.9 mi

❹ Garda

DAY 3

4 km/2.5 mi

❺ Bardolino

5 km/3.1 mi

❻ Lazise

4 km/2.5 mi

❼ Parco Termale del Garda

DAY 4

13 km/8.1 mi

❽ Peschiera

13 km/8.1 mi

❾ Sirmione

13 km/8.1 mi

biking, hiking, surfing or sailing. The next stop is ❸ **Malcesine** → p. 36, which nestles on the shoreline of Lake Garda. An imposing castle towers over the town and delicious ice cream is sold at **Gelateria Cento per Cento** located at the entrance of this fortress.

On the next day, take a boat trip along the eastern shore. **Disembark in ❹ Garda** → p. 56, and take a leisurely walk down the long promenade.

Hop on the bus (no. 62) and head to ❺ **Bardolino** → p. 51. This village is surrounded by rolling vineyards, which are the perfect backdrop for a long walk. In the car-free, medieval city centre of ❻ **Lazise** → p. 61, you can enjoy an aperitif at one of the nice bars around town. But before settling down for the evening, first take a visit to Colà to the Villa dei Cedri with the ❼ **Parco Termale del Garda** → p. 64. This warm thermal lake is surrounded by a wonderful park full of old trees. After a swim, **take the bus back to Lazise.**

Via ❽ **Peschiera** → p. 64, where fortress walls attest to the former strategic position of the town, **continue by boat to ❾ Sirmione** → p. 75 **the next day**. Because of its unique location at the tip of a peninsula, the best way to explore this town is to start from the water. **A short walk will bring you from the dock to the Grotte di Catullo**, one of the most significant Roman excavation sites on the lake, as well as to lovely places to swim. If you stay the night in Sirmione, you can enjoy the town in peace without the hustle and bustle of the many tourists on daytrips. If you prefer a bit more action, then **you should now (or the next morning, if you prefer) head a few miles further to ⑩ Desenzano → p. 70**: The largest town on the lake offers a lively nightlife scene and plenty of shopping to keep you busy the next morning. The elegant town of **⑪ Salò → p. 91**, which is favoured by Italian holidaymakers in particular, lies in a small bay on the southwestern shore. The old town centre with its narrow pedestrian zone and small boutiques stretches behind the longest promenade on the shores of the lake.

The former luxury holiday destination of the Belle Époque, **⑫ Gardone Riviera → p. 81**, attracted the wealthy middle classes at the end of the 19th century and is still one of the most exclusive towns on the lake today. Be sure to check out the famous **Vittoriale degli Italiani**, an impressive residence left behind by the eccentric national poet Gabriele D'Annunzio. You can also marvel at modern art and aged trees in the **Giardino Botanico André Heller**. **Spend the night in the less expensive twin town ⑬ Toscolano-Maderno → p. 85**, which spreads across the fan delta of the torrent Toscolano. For a long time, this municipality was known for its paper manufacturing – if you take a walk along this stream, you can admire the **Valle delle Cartiere** with the INSIDERTIP ruins of its old paper mills.

The affluent town of **⑭ Gargnano → p. 87** with its narrow lanes and colourful houses sits dreamlike along the lakeshore. It has escaped the tourist boom – and if that's what you're looking for, then you can sit back and relax at one of the few cafés along the shore the next morning. At

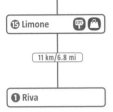

⑮ Limone

11 km/6.8 mi

❶ Riva

the foot of a steep mountain cliff, you will find the charming town of ⑮ **Limone** → p. 32, which is built in terraces above the lakeshore. The houses nestle closely together along the small crooked streets of the picturesque old town centre full of shops. And since the best way to appreciate the beauty of this town is from the water, **you should undertake the last leg of your tour around the lake back to ❶ Riva by ferry**.

2 THE PEAKS OF MONTE BALDO

START: ❶ Monte Baldo cable car top station	5–6 hours
END: ❶ Monte Baldo cable car top station	Walking time (without stops)
Distance: medium difficulty 🔁 3 km/1.9 mi ▫▫▫ Height: 440 m/1444 ft	3.5 hours

COSTS: cable car return fare 20 euros per person
WHAT TO PACK: hiking shoes, rain gear, sun protection, water, packed lunch

IMPORTANT TIPS: you need to be sure-footed and vertigo-free for this medium difficulty hike. *Cable car daily 8am until – depending on the season – 5pm/6pm/7pm | tel. 04 57 40 02 06 | www.funiviedelbaldo.it*

Monte Baldo, which is the highest mountain towering above Lake Garda at a height over 2000 m/6562 ft, is a dream for plant-lovers and an absolute must for hikers and active holidaymakers. Although it is definitely worth the climb, you can travel to the peak in comfort! In a matter of minutes, the panoramic gondola ride will take you from Malcesine to the top station at 1700 m/5577 ft from where you can set off full of energy on this medium difficulty hike. Enjoy wonderful views of Lake Garda and colourful impressions of some rather unusual flora.

09:00am Even the trip up from the cable car station in **Malcesine** → p. 36 is a feast for the eyes. The panoramic gondolas turn as they ascend, offering wonderful views of the lake. Especially in summer, try to get to the lower station as early as possible in order to avoid a long wait. Once you're at the top, take in the fresh mountain air and enjoy the amazing view from the terrace of the ❶ **Monte Baldo cable car top station**. Look to the north to see the wild peaks of the Brenta Dolomites and the snowy crests of Adamello and Presanella. Endless mountain ridges stretch to the south while the lake laps onto the shore far below. You won't be the first to sit down and order a cappuccino

❶ Monte Baldo cable car top station

200 m/656 ft

before taking off on the day's adventure. There is no reason not to enjoy a relaxing start!

The approx. 30 km long/18.6 mi mountain ridge doesn't really have one summit, but rather several high peaks such as Monte Altissimo di Nago (2079 m/6821 ft), Cima delle Pozzette (2132 m/6995 ft), Cima Valdritta (2218 m/7277 ft) and Punta Telegrafo (2200 m/7218 ft). The Cima delle Pozzette is the first peak that you will reach after departing from the cable car station. Although the trail over the crest to this peak is not really difficult, it is demanding enough to make serious trouble for hikers wearing sandals.

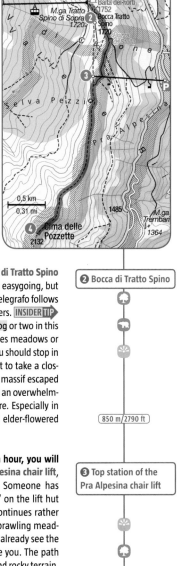

From the cable car station, the trail climbs up slightly and to the right, towards the south, past the cosy inn Baita dei Forti → p. 41. For the entire stretch, you should follow the red-white-red marked path 651 leading down into the trough ❷ **Bocca di Tratto Spino** (1720 m/5643 ft). The trail here is wide and easygoing, but the climb up the other side towards Punta Telegrafo follows a narrow path that slenders through boulders. INSIDER TIP With a bit of luck, you might see a groundhog or two in this area. The trail is in part rocky but also crosses meadows or runs along bushes. Every now and then, you should stop in your tracks and enjoy the view. Don't forget to take a closer look at the flora around you as well. This massif escaped the ice of the last Ice Age, which means that an overwhelming array of flowers and plants flourish here. Especially in May and June, the peonies, tiger lilies and elder-flowered orchids are in full bloom.

10:30am After walking for about half an hour, you will arrive at the ❸ **top station of the Pra Alpesina chair lift**, which connects Monte Baldo with Avio. Someone has sprayed red letters that read "Bel Vedere" on the lift hut – the view is stunning indeed! The trail continues rather evenly over grass-covered ridges, across sprawling meadows and through pine tree groves. You can already see the rugged rocks of Cima delle Pozzette before you. The path alternates between stretches of meadow and rocky terrain.

❷ Bocca di Tratto Spino

850 m / 2790 ft

❸ Top station of the Pra Alpesina chair lift

A real *high*-light at Monte Baldo: the Cima delle Pozzette

After hiking about an hour, you will come across a meadow to the right of the trail that is covered with countless cairns. This is the ideal spot to take a long break and build your own. To the left, you can see the Adige valley and Rovereto below, and to the right Malcesine and the lake.

2350 m / 7710 ft

01:00pm **From here, the trail climbs steadily upwards.** You now need to watch your step; the path leads through bushes and over large boulders, but is mostly dotted with rocks. You will gain height quickly before you come to a rugged ridge and then a saddle. **After about two or two and a half hours, you will reach your destination,** namely **❹ Cima delle Pozzette.** The cross on the summit is a curious feature: a rusty chair frame serves as the holder for a cross made of thick branches, held tight by a few stones and decorated with plastic flowers. The view of the lake about 2000 m/6562 ft below is breathtaking. By now, you have more than earned your sandwich. While tucking into your lunch, study the rocks of Val d'Angual and try to spot the chamois that can sometimes be seen darting over the rocks. **Follow the same trail back down to reach the ❶ Monte Baldo cable car top station in about an hour.**

❹ Cima delle Pozzette

3400 m / 11,155 ft

❶ Monte Baldo cable car top station

THROUGH THE SARCA VALLEY TO TRENTO AND ROVERETO

START: ❶ Torbole
END: ❶ Torbole

Distance:
🚗 approx. 100 km/62 mi

2 days
Driving time
(without stops)
2 hours

COSTS: 27 euros/person for museum admission fees

The Alto Garda region charms visitors with its high mountains, wild rock formations,fruit plantations, vineyards, castles and lakes. Not to mention the delicious Trentino cuisine and spectacular cultural landscape that are waiting to be discovered.It is best to plan two days for this roundtrip tour with its variety of delights.

The route begins in ❶ **Torbole** → p. 45. **After just a few miles,** you will come to the lively town of ❷ **Arco** → p. 48, which is a worthwhile first stop. The pretty old town centre huddles close to a narrow cliff with the ruins of an ancient hilltop castle. In 1872, the Austrian emperor chose this town as the winter residence for his court because of the mild climate. Impressive villas, sweeping promenades and the botanical gardens are the remnants of this imperial past. Today, Arco is a popular destination among outdoor-lovers. Visit the INSIDER TIP Omkafè coffee museum, the **Museo del Caffè** *(Mon–Fri 8am–noon and 2.30pm–6.30pm, Sat 8am–noon | Via Aldo Moro 7 | www.omkafe. com)*, and drink a cup of freshly-brewed coffee!

Continue northwards through the Sarca Valley towards Dro. This region is particularly well-known for its plums as well as *vino santo*, a white dessert wine. After a few bends in the road, you will come to the wild-looking environs of ❸ **Marocche**. In primeval times, a massive landslide hit the valley, leaving enormous rocks scattered about as if giants had been playing with building blocks.

On the left side at the foot of Monte Brento between Dro and Pietramurata, you will find the up to 500 m/1640 ft high so-called "sunny slabs", the **Placche Zebrate**. This is climbing territory, but some climbers also like to drink hot chocolate at ❹ INSIDER TIP **Parete Zebrata** *(Closed Tue |*

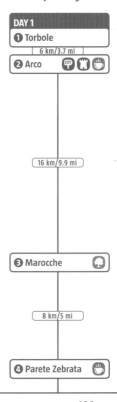

DAY 1
❶ Torbole

6 km/3.7 mi

❷ Arco

16 km/9.9 mi

❸ Marocche

8 km/5 mi

❹ Parete Zebrata

3

Dorsino
San Lorenzo
in Banale
Tavodo Andogno
Ranzo
Margone
Fraveggio
Santa Massenza
Vezzano
Padergnone
Vigolo
Baselga
Lon
Ciago 3,5
CADINE
TRENTO
Stenico
Villa Banale
Seo
Terme di Comano
Comano
Sarche
Calavino
Lago d' Toblino
Lago di Toblino
Bleggio
Lomaso
Monte Casale
Pergolese
Lasino
Cavedine
Brusino
Vigo
Drena
Drena
Dro
Monte Biaina
Ceniga
Vigne
Chiarano
Arco
Bolognano
Nago-
Torbole
Mori
Mori Vecchio

8 km / 5 mi

🍴 **5** Sarche

2 km / 1.2 mi

🏰 **6** Lago di Toblino

Gaggiolo 4 | www.barparetezebrata.it) and observe the activities on the rock face – or watch the free-falling base jumpers who dare to dive off Monte Brento.

Afterwards, continue along the main road to 5 Sarche. Visit the small but well-stocked supermarket at the crossroads to buy yourself a packed lunch. You will find tasty delicacies ranging from pickled asparagus, raspberry jam and bakery goods to cheese and salami. If you ask nicely, one of the employees will make you a *panino* to order. The next stop is just a stone's throw away at **6 Lago di Toblino**. Sitting on an island, **which you can reach on foot by crossing over a dam**, you will find a **moated**

castle with distinctive towers. Originally a 12th-century castle, it was transformed into a comfortable residential palace in the 16th century. Today, it houses a good restaurant: **Ristorante Castel Toblino** *(Closed Tue and Nov–Feb | Via Caffaro 1 | tel. 04 61 86 40 36 | www.casteltoblino.com | Moderate–Expensive)*.

About 20 km/12.4 mi further on, you will come to ❼ **Trento** (pop. 115, 000). For centuries, this beautiful city situated between the Dolomite mountains and Lake Garda has been a melting pot of Italian, German and Austrian culture. It combines the Italian "Dolce Vita" with a dose of central European pragmatism. Let yourself be carried away along the streets of the romantic Old Town and enjoy the palaces, churches and shop windows that await. One of the city's landmarks is the **Baroque Neptune fountain** from 1768 on the **cathedral square**, one of the most beautiful *piazzas* in Italy. For the best view over the heart of the city, head to **Caffè Italia** *(Piazza Duomo 7)*.

Once you have regained your strength, **take a ten-minute walk** to the ★ **Museo delle Scienze MuSe** *(Tue–Fri 10am– 6pm, Sat/Sun 10am–7pm | Corso del Lavoro e della Scienza 3 | www.muse.it)*. In Italy's most modern natural science museum, visitors of all ages can explore the earth from the African bush to the glaciers of the Alps with the help of virtual exhibits. You can also inspect the huge dinosaur skeletons.

For a centrally-located, yet inexpensive place to stay, check out **Hotel Venezia** *(50 rooms | Via Rodolfo Belenzani 70 | tel. 04 61 23 45 59 | www.hotelveneziatn.it | Budget)*. Ask for a room with a view of the cathedral! In the evening, head to **Ristorante al Vò** *(Closed Sun | Vicolo del Vò 11 | tel. 04 61 98 53 74 | www.ristorantealvo.it | Moderate)* – an older restaurant is hard to find as this first Osteria in Trento opened its doors here in 1345; today, the restaurant serves traditional Trentino cuisine. Tourist information: *Via Manci 2 | tel. 04 61 21 60 00 | www.discovertrento.it*

The next day, take SS 12 to ❽ Rovereto (pop. 38,000). Not only the Venetian castle that sits above the lively streets of the old town, but also the mix of Italian Palazzi and Austrian architecture attest to the once strategic position of the town. Until 1919, this town in the Adige Valley belonged to the Austrian Empire and was a bitterly contested city on the front during World War I. For more details about the

17 km/10.6 mi

❼ Trento

DAY 2

❽ Rovereto

town's history during the war, head to the **Museo Storico Italiano della Guerra** *(Tue–Sun 10am–6pm | Via Castelbarco 7 | www.museodellaguerra.it)*.

It is the fusion of history, the present and the future that makes Rovereto so interesting. You can experience this yourself by visiting the ultra-modern museum of modern and contemporary art, the ★ **Museo di Arte Moderna e Contemporanea di Trento e Rovereto MART** *(Tue–Sun 10am–6pm (Fri until 9pm) | Corso Bettini 43 | www.mart.trento.it)*. The main focus of the exhibition is Italian art from the 20th and 21st centuries. The museum also holds one of the most important collections of futuristic art in Italy. The museum itself was designed by the Ticino architect Mario Botta, who was faced with the daunting task of constructing a large modern building in the midst of a densely-built historic city centre. He arranged the three stories of the museum around a huge, round agora topped with a glass dome. This central space can accomodate events with up to 1200 visitors.

It only takes **about 30 minutes on the SS 240** to get back to the lake from Rovereto. **Before the road winds up to the Passo San Giovanni (287 m/941 ft)**, it is well worth a stop first at ❾ **Lago di Loppio**. This protected wetlands area, which only resembles a lake after heavy rainfall, is

16 km/9.9 mi

❾ Lago di Loppio

7 km/4.4 mi

The round agora of Mario Botta's ultra-modern museum building – MART

extremely peaceful and the perfect place to stretch your legs one last time before returning to ❶ **Torbole** → p. 45.

❶ Torbole

4 UP TO THE HEIGHTS OF TREMOSINE AND TIGNALE

START: ❶ Limone END: ❶ Limone	1 day Driving time (without stops) 60–90 minutes
Distance: 🔄 approx. 55 km/34.2 mi	

COSTS: museum admission 5 euros per person
WHAT TO PACK: sturdy shoes

IMPORTANT TIPS: the ❻ **Madonna di Montecastello** *opens daily from Easter–Oct, 9am–6pm; the* ❽ *museum opens March–mid-Dec, Sat–Thu 10am–5pm*

On this diverse day trip, you will explore the sunny municipalities of Tremosine in the Alto Garda Bresciano Nature Park. Nestled between steep canyons and lush meadows, 17 of the 18 quaint villages are situated up to 600 m/1969 ft above the lake and are rarely visited by tourists. What you will find is winding streets, aromatic olive oil, sweet honey and sometimes a truffle or two. A breathtaking road links the Gardesana Occidentale with the main town of Pieve.

10:00am Start off from ❶ **Limone** → p. 32 **and turn right before you reach Campione in the Gardesana Occidentale to head towards Tremosine**. The curvy panoramic road SP 38, known as ❷ ★ **Strada della Forra**, leads through the narrow Brasa canyon up to Pieve. Winston Churchill enthusiastically called this road the "eighth wonder of the world", and Daniel Craig, alias James Bond, filmed a scene from "Quantum of Solace" in front of this impressive backdrop. If you look up to the houses of Pieve from the lake, which stand on a high plateau around 350 m/1148 ft above the water, you can't help but wonder how a road could wind up to this town. It is a true masterpiece of road design and a one-of-a-kind panoramic experience.

After about 2 km/1.2 mi, take your first break. **Just after the canyon narrows considerably, park your car on the left** at Ristorante ❸ **La Forra** *(Closed Tue | Via Benaco 24 | tel. 03 65 91 81 66 | www.laforra.com | Budget)* and

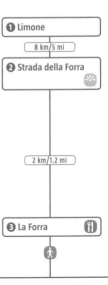

❶ Limone

8 km/5 mi

❷ Strada della Forra

2 km/1.2 mi

❸ La Forra

explore the area on foot. If your stomach is already rumbling, make a pitstop at the restaurant. The pasta is homemade and the beef tenderloin with porcini mushrooms is absolutely delicious.

01:30pm Wait though until you get to nearby **④ Pieve** → p. 89 to enjoy a cup of coffee on one of the two **"swaying terraces"**. The **Hotel Paradiso** sits directly on the edge above the lake and the large terrace sits on top of a platform that juts out from the cliff, offering a view of the lake about 300 m/984 ft directly below. If the weather is rather unpleasant, the nearby Ristorante **Miralago** has a kind of free-floating, panoramic winter garden. Afterwards, it is well worth it to take a stroll through the historic centre of Pieve in which many of the 18th-century houses have been lovingly restored.

If you are a fan of truffles, ask at the tourist information office for Luca – he sometimes has a few of these prized deli-

1 km/0.6 mi

④ Pieve 🌸 ☕ 🚶

8 km/5 mi

Highlight while taking a stroll in Pieve:
a cappuccino on the "swaying terraces"

cacies for sale in autumn. Continue on through the wild hillsides and pine forests, across green plateaus and past olive groves to the cheese dairy **⑤ Alpe del Garda** → p. 90 in Polzone. All the crossroads have signs pointing the way to the dairy. During the summer, INSIDER TIP free tours with a cheese tasting are offered twice daily. There is also a restaurant and a nicely-stocked shop with milk products from the dairy – the raw milk cheese is really good – as well as other local delicacies such as salami, honey and olive oil. It's a good idea to stock up on a packed lunch here!

The panoramic road continues towards Tignale. Far from the hustle and bustle around Lake Garda, this road leads through the untouched mountainous countryside. **Before you reach Gardola, turn left** to

Pilgrims flocked to see the Madonna di Montecastello high above the lake

get to the pilgrimage church **⑥ Madonna di Montecastello** → p. 90, which was built in the 17th century. Like an eagle's nest, it clings to the top of a steep cliff that drops almost 700 m/2297 ft straight down. After taking a look at the church, it is worth hiking about 20 minutes up to the peak of **⑦ Monte Castello. Turn left and go past the church, following the signs "alla croce" to the cross at the top.** Enjoy the unparalleled views of the lake along the path.

04:15pm If you would like to learn more about the Alto Garda Nature Park, you should make one last stop at the small **⑧ museum** → p. 119 in Prabione. It explains how the mountains on the edge of Lake Garda were formed and tells about the lives of the local residents. The nature park is full of contrasts, especially because it stretches from a height of 65 m/213.3 ft on the lakeshore up to a height of almost 2000 m/6562 ft. It is really not surprising that the climate and vegetation, as well as the social and economic factors, vary greatly within the park. **Go through Oldesio and Piovere to head back down to the lake and along Gardesana Occidentale back to ① Limone.**

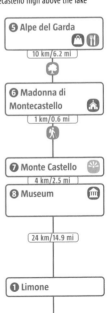

⑤ Alpe del Garda

10 km/6.2 mi

⑥ Madonna di Montecastello

1 km/0.6 mi

⑦ Monte Castello

4 km/2.5 mi

⑧ Museum

24 km/14.9 mi

① Limone

5 BIKING ALONG THE BANKS OF THE MINCIO RIVER

| START: ❶ Peschiera | 1 day |
| END: ❶ Peschiera | Biking time (without stops) approx. 2.5 hours |

| Distance: | easy |
| 🚲 33 km/20.5 mi | 📶 Height: 50 m/164 ft |

COSTS: bike hire 13 euros per person/per day, children 6.50 euros
WHAT TO PACK: drinks and snacks

IMPORTANT TIPS: bike hire *(April–Oct daily 9am–7pm)* near the bike trail: **Noleggio Bici → p. 65**

This some 30 km/18.6 mi bike route follows along the Mincio River through the beautiful countryside between Peschiera and Borghetto di Valeggio sul Mincio. You will come across small cultural and culinary highlights, such as old mills and homemade tortellini, that will turn this day trip into a real adventure for the whole family. The well-marked trail takes you through the Mincio conservation area, which is packed to the gills with waterfowl, fish and anglers.

❶ Peschiera

9 km/5.6 mi

10:00am This tour begins in true Italian style in ❶ Peschiera → p. 64, with a cappuccino and a freshly made brioche (sweet or savory) at **Torta della Nonna** *(Daily | Via Risorgimento 5)*. **Go through the old town centre towards the fortress to get to the river, which is where the bike trail starts.** The Mincio is in fact the only river that drains from Lake Garda, and it flows into the Po River 50 km/31.1 mi to the south near Governolo. Since the river was a natural line of defence in days past, it was of great strategic

Even today the Mincio River still turns the wheels of watermills in idyllic Borghetto

importance for centuries. As you cycle through the quiet countryside with its meadows and vineyards, you will hardly be able to believe that bitter battles took place here during the Italian War of Independence against Austria in the 19th century. But, castles, city walls and watch towers along the riverbanks are testimony to this history.

The well-marked bike path meanders under shady trees through the countryside marked by floodplain forests. Countless species of birds and over 300 kinds of plants flourish along the banks of the river. The white stork was also successfully reintroduced. Many anglers treasure the untouched nature found on these shores.

11:30am After about an hour, the mighty church of the seemingly sleepy village of **❷ Monzambano** arises before you. It is time for a little stop, **so cross over the bridge to follow the path up to the village centre.** Grab a bite to eat at **Caffè Frapporti** (Closed Mon | Piazza Vittorio Emanuele). Enjoy the impressive **INSIDER TIP** view from the watch towers of the Castello over the peaceful riverside to Lake Garda. **Afterwards, hop back on the saddle and return to the bike path.**

12:30pm It won't take much longer before you can see the mighty walls and towers of the 600 m/1969 ft long, fortress-like dam wall **Ponte Visconteo** → p. 63 and the towers of the impressive castle of Valeggio. First, visit the old part of **❸ Borghetto** → p. 63 with its medieval mill district. Time seems to have stood still here, and you can still see the wooden wheels of the watermills. If you are hungry now, cycle on to the neighbouring **❹ Valeggio sul Mincio** and taste the hand-made pasta dishes away from the tourist throng in the **Trattoria Il Cavallino** (Closed Thu | Via Giuseppe Verdi 8 | tel. 04 57 95 11 38 | Moderate). For a dolce, though, you should treat yourself to something sweet at **Pastificio Remelli** (Via Antonio Murari 77). **Then it is time to take the same path back to ❶ Peschiera** → p. 64.

❷ Monzambano

7 km/4.4 mi

❸ Borghetto

1 km/0.6 mi

❹ Valeggio sul Mincio

15 km/9.3 mi

❶ Peschiera

SPORTS & ACTIVITIES

Lake Garda is known and loved for its sports. For decades, the winds have drawn surfers and sailors onto the water. Climbers cherish the limestone walls in the north, which is also home to countless mountain bike trails. The region is chock-full of different hiking and boating options. The mild climate and warm thermal springs also won over the Roman poet Gaius Valerius Catullus who had a thermal bath built in his villa in Sirmione around 2000 years ago.

CANYONING

It is not possible to indulge in some kinds of adventure sports without professional instruction. Canyoning is one of them. The following establishments

provide guided tours: *XMountain (Via Frà Giovanni da Schio 1e | San Giovanni Lupatoto | tel. 34 81 46 37 00 | www. xmountain.it); Canyon Adventures (Via Matteotti 122 | Torbole | tel. 33 48 69 86 66 | www.canyonadv.com);* INSIDER TIP *Mmove (Via Legionari Cecolsovacci 14 | tel. 33 81 93 33 74 | www.mmove.net); Skyclimber (Via Dalco 3 | Tremosine | tel. 3 35 29 32 37 | www.skyclimber.it)*

CLIMBING & BOULDERING

Apparently, the cradle of European climbing sports is in Arco. It's true that there are over 2000 climbing routes that cater for practically every difficulty level. Those who prefer not to climb solo can join the local mountain guides

An adventure playground for adults: water sports fans and mountain lovers can really let off steam on Lake Garda

– the spectrum ranges from fun climb to climbing for children and all types of courses. When the weather is stormy or it rains, an alternative is ● *Bouldercity (Sept–July Mon–Fri 10am–11pm, Sat/Sun depending on weather | Viale Daino 74a | Pietramurata | www. bouldercity.it)* in the Sarca Valley. The climbing competition held in late summer in Arco, *Rock Master (www.rockmaster.com)*, is a spectacular experience for onlookers and attracts the world's elite among free climbers.

CYCLING & MOUNTAIN BIKING

The north is the most popular area for ambitious cyclists. The trail *Mountain & Garda Bike (www.mountaingardabike. com)* stretches over 218 km/135 mi and climbs a total of 10,000 m (32,808 ft). The *Bike Festival (www.riva.bike-festival. de)* is held around Riva in late April/ early May.
● Monte Baldo is the most popular destination among fit mountain bikers.

Those who want to avoid the grind of riding uphill take the cable car from Malcesine, INSIDER TIP which also transports bikes at certain times. You can not only hire bikes from *Xtreme* at the cable car station in the valley *(Via Navene Vecchia 10 | tel. 04 57 40 01 05 | www.xtrememalcesine.com)*, they will even transport them to the top of Monte Baldo.

The province of Verona has introduced the *Bus & Bike service (tel. 04 58 05 79 22)* for the summer months: you take the scheduled bus service, which also transports bikes, from Garda up to San Zeno di Montagna or Prada on the slopes of Monte Baldo, and from there it is downhill all the way.

If you're looking for a more relaxed way to explore the lake on a bike, try the different trails through the countryside along the shore. Although it is still not possible to cycle around the entire lake, new stretches of the trail are opening every year.

DIVING

Diving centres offering courses and tours can be found in Torri del Benaco, Riva, Salò and Desenzano. *Arco Sub (tel. 34 00 04 56 51 | www.arcosub.com)* in Torbole organises courses.

HIKING

You just walked past a castle, paused to rest beneath an olive tree – and now you are already standing between rugged rock formations before heading across expansive mountain meadows: these contrasts account for the charm of hiking along Lake Garda. The most beautiful areas are Monte Baldo on the east shore, the Alto Garda Bresciano nature park on the west shore, Ledro Valley and

Lake Tenno in the north and Rocca di Garda, Mincio Valley and Rocca di Manerba in the south.

The *Sentiero della Pace* is worth seeing and extends for over 500 km/311 mi from the Stelvio Pass as far as Marmolada along the front line of the First World War. It links ramparts and fortress sites, tunnels and cemeteries as well as large and small museums. The southern part between Riva and Rovereto *(short.travel/gar20)* with Monte Brione is easily accessible. The impressions of the countryside along this hiking trail are often spectacular, however, thoughtful hikers will be reminded at every step of the terrible events that occurred along the route. An estimate of the victims who fell in the mountains during the war from 1915 to 1918 is up to 150,000 or 180,000 soldiers on both sides.

JOGGING & TRAIL RUNNING

Are you a keen jogger? Don't forget your running shoes, as the lakeside promenades, pebbly routes, paths and trails around the lake are a genuine paradise for joggers. Those with a competitive streak can choose from the following options: *Lake Garda Marathon (www.lakegardamarathon.com)*, skyrunning in the *Limone Extreme Skyrace (www.limonextreme.com)* or the *Garda Trentino Half Marathon (www.trentinoeventi.it)*.

RIDING

Riding and horseback tours are organised by *Ranch Il Bosco (Puegnago sul Garda | tel. 03 65 55 55 05 | www.ranchilbosco.it)*; *Scuderia Castello (Toscolano-Maderno | tel. 03 65 64 41 01 | www.scuderiacastello.it)*; *Club Ippico San Giorgio Arco (tel. 34 84 43 83 07 | www.clubippicosangiorgio.it)*.

SAILING

Since the 1960s Lake Garda has been one of Europe's most popular sailing locations thanks to its constant winds. There are sailing schools everywhere on the lake. Every year almost 100 regattas are held, the most famous is certainly the *Centomiglia (www.centomiglia.it)* in September in Bogliaco.

WELLNESS

The lake has a unique micro-climate and thermal springs bubble deeply within the rocks. This is a great recipe for a good dose of relaxation and pampering. In addition to the thermal spas in Sirmione *(www.termedisirmione.com)*, Lazise *(www.villadeicedri.it)* and Santa Lucia di Pescantina *(www.aquardens.it)* or at the Lido di Arco *(www.gardathermae.it)*, many accommodations are also increasing the number of wellness options.

WIND- & KITESURFING

The supreme discipline on Lake Garda, which is particularly well suited for windsurfing because its northern section emerges from a narrow mountain valley through which regular winds blow like from a jet. Torbole on the north shore is the surfers' Mecca; in Riva, the conditions are also suitable for beginners. One more advantage of the northern lake corner: motorboats are not permitted in the Trentino section of the lake. In addition to Torbole, the surfing schools renting boards are mainly concentrated in Riva, Malcesine and Gargnano. Kitesurfing is quickly gaining in popularity. Most surf schools have included this trendy sport in their portfolio.

Without doubt: windsurfing is the no. 1 sport on Lake Garda

TRAVEL WITH KIDS

A holiday on Lake Garda means a good dose of splashing fun, nature and entertainment for the whole family. If someone wants to surf, but others want to go climbing or hiking or just sit back and relax, this is easily arranged at Lake Garda. Or maybe you are looking for a mix of roller coasters and alpine meadows with an art museum or climbing park thrown in, plus cycling and swimming? There are countless possibilities for a fun family holiday on Lake Garda.

The north shore is a good place for older children – they can try their hand at surfing or sailing as well as climbing and canyoning in a kid-friendly environment. In the south on the other hand, the lake is so shallow that parents can calmly let their offspring splash around. The following beaches are particularly suitable for children: the *Punta Cornicello* in Bardolino (small, but with trees and a playground), the *beach near the port in Pacengo* (flat sandy beach, a few trees, paddle-boat hire, showers and a bar), *Lido di Ronchi* (flat sandy beach with grassy areas and trees, a bar and showers) not far from Gardaland, as well as the *Spiaggia Comunale* in Santa Maria di Lugana near the Sirmione peninsula (wide stretch of grassy shoreline, playground). On the north shore in the centre of Riva, the large *Spiaggia Sabbiono* (lots of trees, pebbly beach, artificial bathing islands, playgrounds, bars) beckons.

Safari, aquatic and amusement parks provide a change. But don't forget the range of things the lake naturally has to offer!

EAST SHORE

CANEVAWORLD (142 C4) (*∅ H7*)

In the leisure park Carnevaworld at the southern end of Lazise with its water park, Movieland, Rock Café and "Mister Movie Studios", there is also a restaurant with medieval shows. *June–mid Sept daily 10am–6pm (mid July–mid Aug until 7pm/11pm), April/May and mid-Sept–Oct sporadic opening days | 28 euros, children under 1.40 m/4 ft 7 in 22 euros, up to 1 m/3 ft 3.5 in free, reduced prices online |* *Lazise | located in Fossalta 58 | www.canevaworld.it*

GARDACQUA (142 C3) (*∅ H6*)

Is the weather changeable? Visit the swimming pool! The Gardacqua in Garda has several indoor and outdoor pools, a wellness area and summer area with sun loungers, olive trees and pool with water games and a slide. *Daily 9am–8pm | Day ticket 8.50 euros, Sat/Sun 9.50 euros, children (3–14 years) 6.90/7.90 euros | Via Cirillo Salaorni 10 | www.gardacqua.eu*

GARDALAND (142 C5) (*Ⓜ H8*)

The oldest amusement park on Lake Garda offers traditional entertainment à la Disneyland and has many attractions for all age groups: the adventurous take a ride on the legendary Raptor roller coaster or the Blue Tornado. The littlest visitors can explore Prezzemolo Land with is fairytale castle surrounded by fun-filled water slides. The park is often hopelessly overcrowded in summer and your patience will already be tested on the approach roads. *Opening times vary considerably. Daily April–Sept, generally 10am–6pm, Oct–Jan sometimes 10am–6pm, daily mid June–mid Sept 10qm–11pm | 40.50 euros, children (>1 m/3 ft 3.5 in–9 years) 34 euros, reduced prices online | www.gardaland.it*

JUNGLE ADVENTURE PARK
(142 C2) (*Ⓜ H5*)

Clamber around the tree canopy on wooden boardwalks in this aerial ropeway and adventure park above San Zeno di Montagna. *May–mid Sept daily 10am–8pm, April and mid Sept–Oct Sat/Sun 10am–7pm | depending on the route chosen 8–34 euros | www.jungleadventure.it*

PARCO NATURA VIVA (143 D5) (*Ⓜ J7*)

You can watch rhinoceroses, lions and tigers in the wild, from the safety of your car, in this safari park, located between Pastrengo and Bussolengo in the area beyond Lazise. You must however keep the windows closed! A total of more than 280 animal species live here. Visitors are catapulted millions of years into the past in Extinction Park. New ideas and life-like replicas tell the evolutionary history of the dinosaurs. *Daily March–Nov, opening times vary, but generally from around 9am–6pm | combined tickets for Safari Park and Zoo 20 euros, children under 12, 15 euros | www.parconaturaviva.it*

RIOVALLI (143 D4) (*Ⓜ H7*)

Those who are not satisfied with just bathing and hanging around can travel

Gardaland on the east shore: a magnet for the young and young at heart between 2 and 70!

to the Riovalli aquatic park on the outskirts of Bardolino. *Mid–June–mid-Sept Mon–Fri 9.30am–7pm, Sat/Sun 9am–7pm | 9 euros (Sat 9.50 euros, Sun 10.50 euros), children (3–12 years) 7 euros (Sat 7.50 euros, Sun 8 euros) | Cavaion Veronese | in Fosse on the main road near Affi | www.riovalli.it*

SEA LIFE GARDALAND ●
(142 C5) (*Ⓜ H8*)

The large aquarium on the same site as the leisure park shows what's going on in the world's oceans but also in Lake Garda. The 35 main basins are alive with crabs and starfish, sharks and rays. Sealions can also be seen in one of the outdoor basins as can a coral reef. *Daily April–Sept 10am–6pm, considerably varying opening days and times in winter | 16 euros, children (> 1m (3ft 3.5in)–9 years) 10.50 euros, reduced prices online | www.gardaland.it*

NORTH SHORE

MUSEO DELLE PALAFITTE
(137 E3) (*Ⓜ H2*)

At the lake dwelling museum in Molina di Ledro on Lake Ledro above Riva, children and grown-ups alike marvel at what the archaeologists have excavated from the peaty mud near the shore – even including leftover food! *March–June and Sept–Nov Tue–Sun 9am–5pm, July/Aug daily 9am–6pm | 3.50 euros, children 2.50 euros | www.palafitteledro.it*

OUTDOOR ACTION FOR KIDS
(138 C3) (*Ⓜ J2*)

The climbing school *Mmove (Via Legionari Cecoslovacchi 14 | tel. 33 81 93 33 74 | www.mmove.net)* in Arco offers a two-hour children's climbing course several times a week and several climbing courses as well as a versatile weekly programme for all the family.

REPTILAND (138 C3) (*Ⓜ J2*)

This reptile house is located in the old town centre of Riva. Powerful pythons, poisonous snakes and scorpions await safely behind glass. *Daily 11am–8pm | 8 euros, children 7 euros, up to 8 years free | Piazza Garibaldi 2 | www.reptiland.it*

WIND-SURFING COURSE FOR KIDS
(138 C3–4) (*Ⓜ J2*)

The Vasco Renna surfing school in Torbole offers courses with equipment specially designed for children. *Tel. 04 64 50 59 93 | www.vascorenna.com*

SOUTH SHORE

LA FATTORIA DIDATTICA (0) (*Ⓜ 0*)

This historic farm in the *Parco Giardino Sigurtà* has been adapted into a teaching farm with native breeds of chicken, duck and turkey, and donkeys and sheep from the Lessini mountains in the area. *Daily March–Sept 9am–6pm, Oct/Nov 9am–5pm| 12.50 euros, children (5–14 years) 6.50 euros | Valeggio sul Mincio | www.sigurta.it*

WEST SHORE

MUSEO DEL PARCO ALTO GARDA BRESCIANO – CENTRO VISITATORI
(137 E5) (*Ⓜ H4*)

The perfect programme for a rainy day: the geology, flora, fauna and life in the region are explained in this brand-new well-laid out museum. Ask for the English translations at the reception desk. *Mid-April–Oct Sun–Fri 10am–noon and 3pm–5pm (Sun 2pm–5pm) | 5 euros, children under 14 years 4 euros | Tignale | located in Prabione*

FESTIVALS & EVENTS

In the high season there are any number of festivals and celebrations going on. Keep an eye out for posters or just ask at the tourist information office.

FESTIVALS & EVENTS

EASTER
A candle-lit procession depicting the *Passion of Christ* takes place at night on *Venerdì Santo (Good Friday)* in the Old Town in Limone and the Stations of the Cross are visited in the form of a *Passion play* in Castelletto di Brenzone.

LATE APRIL/EARLY MAY
Bike festival (riva.bike-festival.de) in Riva. *Fish & Chef (www.fishandchef.it)* in Malcesine and other places on the eastern shore: celebrity chefs put their cooking to the test in renowned hotels.

MAY
The 1000-mile-rally *Mille Miglia (www. 1000miglia.eu)*, which runs from Brescia to Rome and back, is a homage to days gone by.

LATE MAY/EARLY JUNE
Bardolino celebrates Rosé wines at the large *Palio del Chiaretto*.

JUNE
Every year, San Martino della Battaglia holds the *Rievocazione Storica della Battaglia di Solferino e San Martino*, which is a re-enactment of the historic battle that took place here in 1895. *www.solferinoesanmartino.it*

The Visconti bridge in Valeggio sul Mincio is turned into a large open-air restaurant to celebrate the traditional "love knots" known as tortellini during the INSIDER TIP ▸ *Festa del Nodo d'Amore*.

JULY
Every year, Garda celebrates the lake's sardines for a whole day with the traditional festival *Sardellata al Chiar di Luna*.

JULY/AUGUST
In the summer, *concerts* take place in many towns on the lake, for example (already from June) the *Garda Jazz Festival (www.gardajazz.com)* in the region Alto Garda, the concerts in the theatre Vittoriale degli Italiani *(www.anfiteatrodelvittoriale.it)*, the *Estate Musicale del Garda (www.gardalombardia.com)* or the *concert summer Monte Baldo (www.funiviedelbaldo.it)*.

The prize-winning performing arts festival *Drodesera Fies Festival (www.*

centralefies.it) in an old hydroelectric power station in Dro offers young artists a chance to make a name for themselves. Verona's arena plays host to the annual *Opera Festival* (www.arena.it).

At the *Aperitivo sotto le stelle* (www.degustibus.org) – "Aperitif under the stars" in Bardolino, the lakeside promenade is transformed into a lounge bar that extends for 200 m/656 ft.

For four days and nights the INSIDER TIP *Notte di Fiaba* (www.nottedifiaba.it) transforms Riva into a fairy tale land with theatre, music, fun and entertainment. The highlight is the massive firework display.

SEPTEMBER
International dance groups come together at the *Oriente Occidente* (www.orienteoccidente.it) dance festival in Rovereto and Trento.

The biggest sailing regatta on Lake Garda, the *Centomiglia* (www.centomiglia.it) starts in Gargnano.

SEPTEMBER/OCTOBER
At the end of September/beginning of October, the *Festa dell'Uva e del Vino*, a wine festival with cult status, takes place in Bardolino and Malcesine hosts the culinary festival *Ciottolando con Gus-*

to (www.ciottolando.com) with wine tastings and food stations. The *Festa del Marrone di San Zeno* in San Zeno is dedicated to chestnuts.

OCTOBER
In mid-October thousands of runners from around the world gather to participate in the *Lake Garda Marathon*. www.lakegardamarathon.com

PUBLIC HOLIDAYS

1 Jan	*Capodanno*
6 Jan	*Epifania*
March/April	*Pasqua* and *Pasquetta* (Easter Sunday and Easter Monday)
25 April	*Liberazione* (Anniversary of the liberation from fascism)
1 May	*Festa del Lavoro*
2 June	*Festa della Repubblica* (National holiday)
15 Aug	*Ferragosto*
1 Nov	*Ognissanti*
8 Dec	*Immacolata Concezione*
25 Dec	*Natale*
26 Dec	*Santo Stefano*

LINKS, BLOGS, APPS & MORE

LINKS & BLOGS

www.garda-outdoors.com A well-designed and up-to-date blog with all the news from the lake – unfortunately, so far it is only available in Italian

www.gardagreentourism.eu/en The Green Line Project is an initiative, which supports rural and close-to-nature tourism

www.gardalombardia.com is an excellent site with information about the places on the western shore (the Lombard coast) from Limone to Desenzano. It has listings for hotels, restaurants, cultural events, sports and wellness as well as webcams from each of the villages and some online maps.

www.gardatrentino.it/en/lake-garda A site run by a consortium of villages on the northern coast to promote the hospitality industry in their area. The site includes special offers, suggested routes, themed holidays, weather updates as well as the usual accommodation, events and restaurant listings.

http://www.visitgarda.com/en/garda_lake is the official tourism website of Lake Garda. The listings include hotels, apartments, holiday farms and camp sites.

www.gardapass.com/index.cfm/en is an online hotel booking site specialising in the east coast area. It also has other useful information about internal transport links, local museums and places of interest.

www.lake-garda-revealed.com A good site for tips and up to the minute details on activities around the lake. The site has lots of links to other web pages, topical news and a forum with a FAQ section.

www.gardalake.com Overview site for the Lake Garda region – accomodation (from hotels to camping and farm holidays), restaurants, maps, sightseeing, activities.

short.travel/gar5 Photo gallery with professional photos that you can also purchase

Regardless of whether you are still preparing your trip or already on Lake Garda: these addresses will provide you with more information, videos and networks to make your holiday even more enjoyable.

www.facebook.com/lakegarda Lake Garda on Facebook

blog.gardatrentino.it/en Official blog from the Tourist Office updates you with interesting information about the north shore

short.travel/gar13 Surfers – who occasionally fall into the water

short.travel/gar10 Join the ride: a breathtaking motorbike trip through Brasa canyon from Pieve to Limone

VIDEOS & MUSIC

short.travel/gar16 Video with Adam Ondra, the Czech world-class climber. In Italian, with fabulous pictures

short.travel/gar14 Video about André Heller's botanic garden in Gardone

short.travel/gar15 A guided canyoning tour through the Rio Nero Canyon in Ledro Valley

short.travel/gar23 Now slightly outdated, but still a cool video for kite-surfers and fans of Lake Garda

short.travel/gar24 A must for all bikers: downhill from Tremalzo Pass – a laid-back video from a helmet camera

short.travel/gar25 Atmospheric video about the Marocche di Dro, one of Europe's biggest landslide areas

Lake Garda GPS bike guide With this App, you will always find the correct route

APPS

Lake Garda Trentino Guide The most comprehensive guide for the Trentino side of the lake. iPhone and iPad, free.

Garda App Details of some familiar routes, this App takes mountain-bikers, climbers, surfers and sailors to their hot spots. Also, tips for eating and shopping. Ideal to prepare for your holiday

TRAVEL TIPS

ARRIVAL

People coming from the north take the route via Austria and the Brenner Pass. Those wanting to save the toll charges, or who prefer to travel more leisurely, can take the old Brenner Pass route. There are two possibilities from Trento: you can drive down into the Sarca Valley and approach Lake Garda via Arco and Riva. Or, drive to the Rovereto South motorway exit and reach Torbole by way of Nago. Pleasant advantage: for the last few miles after Nago, there is a wonderful view of the lake for you to enjoy. Those heading for the southern section of the lake take the motorway exit Affi near Bardolino and Garda. Holidaymakers travelling through southwest Germany and Switzerland reach Lake Garda along the Gotthard motorway and then the Milan–Venice motorway (exit: Desenzano, Sirmione and Peschiera). You need a vignette if you use the Swiss and Austrian motorways (for ten days or two months, one legal year in Switzerland); route-bound tolls are levied on motorways in Italy.

The quickest way from Britain by train is with the Eurostar via Paris and then on to Milan. IC and Eurocity trains link other European cities with main Italian destinations. Italy's dense rail network, reasonable ticket prices and reliable train schedules make travelling by rail an excellent way of getting around.
In Rovereto, you can transfer to the public bus service, which will take you directly to the north shore of Lake Garda. From Verona, take the train to Milan and get off in Peschiera or Desenzano. For further information: www.europeanrail.com, www.eurostar.com, www.trainitalia.com and www.raileurope.co.uk

You can travel from England to Lake Garda by bus, e.g. from Birmingham via London to Pescheria. The duration of the journey is 29 hours. www.rome2rio.com

Verona's Valerio Catullo (www.aeroportoverona.it) is the closest airport to Lake Garda. A number of airlines offer regular flights from cities around the UK to Verona. You can also fly to Venice, Milan or Bergamo. No trains run from Verona airport into the city, but the aerobus runs every 20 minutes from the terminal to Verona's main station Porto Nuova. A single ticket costs 6 euros. Trains run from the main station to Trento, Rovereto and Lake Garda. From mid-July to mid-September, bus 164 runs hourly along the eastern short via Peschiera to Garda (connections to Riva); a single ticket costs 3.40–5.80 euros, depending on destination (www.atv.verona.it). There are also private shuttle services,

RESPONSIBLE TRAVEL

It doesn't take a lot to be environmentally friendly whilst travelling. Don't just think about your carbon footprint whilst flying to and from your holiday destination but also about how you can protect nature and culture abroad. As a tourist it is especially important to respect nature, look out for local products, cycle instead of driving, save water and much more. If you would like to find out more about eco-tourism please visit: www.ecotourism.org

From arrival to weather

e.g. Europlan *(www.europlan.it/transfer)* or Lake Garda Transfer *(www.lakegardatransfer.com)*, many hotels and campsites offer their own airport shuttle service.

BEACHES

Lake Garda beaches are usually pebbly and not very wide. Water quality and swim safety are monitored during the official season from May to September. Dogs are not always welcome; and the same applies for fans of nudist beaches. On the east and west shores, the beaches are often narrow or located below the main road. The broad beaches of *Sabbioni*, *Porfina* and *dei Pini* stretch for about 1.5 km/0.9 mi to the east of Riva. They have sunbathing lawns, bars, toilets, showers and playgrounds. The popular *Spiaggia di Paina* is located in the north of Malcesine before Retelino. Most of the bays of Brenzone are quite narrow and less suitable for families with small children. Pretty places to swim in this area can be found in Cassone and Castelletto. A nature reserve with reeds, lots of birds and peaceful sunbathing areas lies between Garda and Bardolino. The long, flat pebble beach *Spiaggia del Corno* in Garda bustles with life, and it is a good place to go with kids. The broadest beaches are between Lazise and Peschiera – some even have sand – with relatively shallow water and well-organised activities. In summer, these beaches are often crowded. A real classic among the Lake Garda beaches is *Lido delle Bionde* in Sirmione below the Roman ruins. The long beaches around Manerba are very popular with families. The prettiest beach in Limone, *Spiaggia Cola*, is located south of the car park and has toilets, restaurants and bars.

BUSES

It cannot be repeated enough: leave your car in the hotel carpark and use public transport! The roads around the lake are chronically jammed. The bus trip from Riva to Limone does not even cost 2 euros – parking in Limone costs 1 euro an hour. Bus timetables can be obtained from all tourist offices and the buses are fairly punctual – traffic permitting. Tickets *(biglietti)* have to be bought before the start of the journey; in the larger villages from the ticket office at the bus station or else from tobacconists. You can also buy one on the bus – but you will have to pay almost double. *www.ttspa.it, www.atv.verona.it, www.trasportibrescia.it*

CAMPING

Not all shores around Lake Garda are equally suitable for camping; there is too little space in the north due to the sheer rock faces. Most camp sites are in the south, especially in Valtenesi between Desenzano and Salò, and most are of a good standard. The price per night is usually around 13 euros for the site, 9 euros for each adult and 7 euros for each child.

CAR HIRE

There are car-rental firms *(autonoleggio)* – both the big international and local companies – in many towns around the lake. It is recommended that you book in advance for the high season.

CLIMATE, WHEN TO GO

In winter, the temperature seldom dips below freezing point. Only a few hotels are open but this is when the west shore displays its fin-de-siècle charm. When there is snow in the mountains and fog lies on the damp Po plain, you may still be able to go for a walk in the sun on Lake Garda. Spring is perhaps the best time to visit Lake Garda: the mild climate is perfect for hiking, the hotel prices are still moderate (except at Easter) and you can easily find somewhere to stay. In summer it can get hot although the wind off the lake makes the temperature more bearable. The one drawback is that everyone in northern Italy seems to spend their holidays here. Weekends in August is bumper-to-bumper time: mile-long traffic jams with stop-and-go on the roads and body contact on the beaches. Autumn is perfect for hiking. Weeks of stable weather are not unusual and from the top of Monte Baldo you can see from the glaciers to Verona.

CUSTOMS

Travellers from other EU countries are no longer subject to custom checks. There are some standard values like 10 l of spirits and 800 cigarettes. Duty-free for non-EU citizens are: 2 l of wine, 1 l of spirits and 200 cigarettes. US and Canadian customs authorities have details of respective limits for goods brought back from abroad. When flying into Italy, non-EU citizens require an onward or return ticket.

DRIVING

The maximum speed in built-up areas is 50 km/h (30 mph), on main roads 90 km/h (56 mph), on dual carriageways 110 km/h (68 mph) and 130 km/h (81 mph) on motorways. It is mandatory to drive with dipped headlights outside of built-up areas during the day; this applies to motorbike and moped riders everywhere. The blood alcohol limit is 0.5. There must be an emergency jacket for each passenger in the car which has to be worn when leaving the car due to a breakdown or an accident outside of built-up areas. Italy cracks down on traffic offenders and there are very strict rules to be observed: alcohol is absolutely prohibited under the age of 21 and during the first three years of someone possessing a driving licence. Those who have just passed their test are not allowed to drive faster than 90 km/h (56 mph) on main roads or 100 km/h (62 mph) on motorways. Anyone cycling after dark outside of built-up areas must wear a high-visibility jacket or warning stripes. Charges are almost always levied when parking in a town and the police hand out tickets with great enthusiasm. With the exception of those located on motorways, most petrol stations close for lunch and on Sundays, although many do have credit card-operated pumps. Breakdown service (toll-free number): *tel. 80 31 16.*

EMBASSIES & CONSULATES

BRITISH CONSULATE GENERAL
Via S. Paolo 7 | Milan | tel. 02 72 30 01 | www.gov.uk/government/world/orga nisations/british-embassy-rome/office/ british-consulate-general-milan

U.S. CONSULATE GENERAL
Via Principe Amedeo 2/10 | Milan | tel. 02 29 03 51 | it.usembassy.gov/embassy consulates/milan

EMBASSY OF CANADA
Via Zara 30 | Rome | tel. 06 85 44 41 | http://www.canadainternational.gc.ca/ italy-italie/index.aspx?lang=eng

EMERGENCY SERVICES

General emergencies *tel. 112*; medical emergencies and mountain rescue *tel. 118*; police *tel. 113*; fire brigade *tel. 115*

ENTRANCE FEES

At tourist attractions like the MART in Rovereto, the Giardino Botanico André Heller or Vittoriale in Gardone expect to pay 11–16 euros. For the Grotte di Catullo or the castle in Sirmione as well as for Cascata del Varone in Riva, entry costs 5–6 euros. Amusement parks like Gardaland (from 37 euros) are expensive. In many museums youngsters and seniors have free entry (under 12 and over 60).

You can save money with the ● *Garda Promotions Card.* You get reductions in musuems and leisure parks, such as Vittoriale, Parco Natura Viva, the Arena in Verona, Gardaland and Canevaworld. Reductions are also given for boat trips and the cable car in Malcesine. The card is available for free in tourist offices and most hotels.

FERRIES

● The ferries Maderno–Torri del Benaco (every hour by day) and Limone–Malcesine (10 times a day) save you driving half way round half the lake. During the peak season a car ferry operates between Riva–Desenzano and back, only stopping at a few places. Passenger ferries between Desenzano and Riva stop at many places en route. In the summer season, evening cruises a held. Timetables are available from the tourist information offices and where the boats come in where you can also buy tickets (in advance). *www.navlaghi.it*

HEALTH

The least complicated method: in case of illness, pay for your doctor and medicine on the spot and present your bills to the health service when you return home for problem-free reimbursement. The new European Health Insurance Card (EHIC) is also accepted. During the summer season the emergency doctor, the *Guardia Medica Turistica* is on standby and looks after holidaymakers.

BUDGETING

Coffee	1.30–2.65 £/1.70–3.35 $
	for a cappuccino
Snack	from 3.10 £/3.90 $
	for a filled panino
Wine	0.90–1.60 £/1.10–2 $
	for 0,1 l at a bar
Olive oil	from 12 £/17 $
	for 1 litre olio extravergine
Petrol	around 1.35 £/1.75 $
	for 1 litre Super Euro 95
Cable car	19.50 £/24.50 $
	for a return trip up and down Monte Baldo

IMMIGRATION

Visas are not required for EU citizens; citizens of the US or Canada require a visa only if staying for longer than three months. A valid identity card or passport is sufficient to allow entry to Italy.

INFORMATION

ITALIAN GOVERNMENT TOURIST BOARD ENIT

In the UK: *1, Princes Street, W1B 2AY London, tel. 020-7408 1254;* in the US: *630, Fifth Avenue – Suite 1965, New York, NY, 10111, tel. 212-245 48 22;* in Canada: *110 Yonge Street – Suite 503, Toronto M5C 1T4, tel. 416-925 48 82. www.enit.it*

INFORMATIVE WEBSITES

The official joint tourism website for the regions of Trentino, Veneto and Lombardy is *www.visitgarda.com*. Detailed travel information about the lake, the surrounding countryside and select accommodations in the different regions is also available at *www.gardalombardia. com*, *www.gardatrentino.it* and *www. lagodigardaveneto.com*.

INTERNET & WIFI

It is no longer just the major hotels that provide WiFi as many municipalities have set up hotspots. Free Luna *(www.futur3. it)* is a free network covering the northern Lake Garda region. Bardolino provides free access for those who have an Italian SIM card through the *Comune di Bardolino* network; all others have to register with a credit card and pay 3 euros per day or 10 euros per week. If you want unlimited Internet access, the best thing to do is to buy an Italian SIM card with which you can surf the web for a month. They cost about 12 euros for a volume of 2 GB and 25 euros for 10 GB.

MONEY & CREDIT CARDS

Cash dispenser are available everywhere and the usual credit cards are accepted at petrol stations, virtually all hotels, most restaurants and in many shops.

NEWSPAPERS

English-language newspapers and magazines are available at many kiosks. You might get European editions of *The Guardian* and *Financial Times* as well as

WEATHER IN RIVA

	Jan	Feb	March	April	May	June	July	Aug	Sept	Oct	Nov	Dec
Daytime temperatures in °C/°F	5/41	7/45	12/54	17/63	20/68	24/75	27/81	26/79	22/72	16/61	11/52	6/43
Nighttime temperatures in °C/°F	1/34	1/34	4/39	9/48	13/55	17/63	19/66	18/64	15/59	10/50	5/41	2/36
Sunshine hours/day	3	4	5	5	6	7	8	7	6	6	3	3
Precipitation days/month	5	5	7	9	11	10	8	8	7	8	8	6
Water temperature	8/46	6/43	8/46	10/50	13/55	18/64	20/68	21/70	19/66	16/61	12/54	10/50

an Italian edition of the *International Herald Tribune* or *USA Today*.

OPENING HOURS

Opening hours are not uniformly regulated in Italy but shops are usually open Mon–Sat 9am–noon and 3.30pm–7pm; larger supermarkets usually have no lunch break. In many towns the shops in the pedestrian precincts are open until 10pm. Most grocery stores are also open on Sunday morning.

PHONE & MOBILE PHONE

The country code for Italy is 0039. You have to to dial the 0 at the beginning of each fixed-line connection – both from abroad and when making local calls. Mobile telephone numbers (often 338 or 339) are always dialled without 0. Country codes from Italy are 0044 (UK), 001 (US and Canada) and 00353 (Ireland). 170 or 172 followed by the country code will connect you to an operator in your home country and allows you to make international collect calls. Telephone cards can be purchased in most *tabacchi* shops. Most British mobile phones work without a problem in Italy. With an Italian prepaid card (available at kiosks or phone shops), incoming calls are free.

POST

Stamps *(francobolli)* are available from post offices, tobacconists *(tabacchi)* but hardly ever where you buy postcards.

PRICES

If you want to enjoy your cappuccino with a view of the lake, be prepared to pay twice as much as at the bar. If you want to eat more than a pizza (about 6.50 euros) and order in true Italian style – *antipasti* or pasta, main course, wine and dessert – count on at least 30–40 euros per person. It will be hard to find a double room for less than 60 euros.

TIPPING

A fixed service charge is generally included in the bill. This charge generally replaces the more usual tip in Italy. On Lake Garda, however, the northern tradition for tipping and the Italian custom of charging a *coperto* have been combined, so that a tip is more usual but by no means expected. First, always ensure you receive your change. Then you can leave the tip on the little tray with the bill.

CURRENCY CONVERTER

£	€	€	£
1	1.15	1	0.88
3	3.45	3	2.64
5	5.75	5	4.40
13	14.95	13	11.44
40	46	40	35.20
75	86.25	75	66
120	138	120	105.60
250	287.50	250	220
500	575	500	440

$	€	€	$
1	0.90	1	1.10
3	2.70	3	3.30
5	4.50	5	5.50
13	11.70	13	14.30
40	36	40	44
75	67.50	75	82.50
120	108	120	132
250	225	250	275
500	450	500	550

For current exchange rates see www.xe.com

USEFUL PHRASES ITALIAN

PRONUNCIATION

c, cc	before e or i like ch in "church", e.g. ciabatta, otherwise like k
ch, cch	like k, e.g. pacchi, che
g, gg	before e or i like j in "just", e.g. gente, otherwise like g in "get"
gl	like "lli" in "million", e.g. figlio
gn	as in "cognac", e.g. bagno
sc	before e or i like sh, e.g. uscita
sch	like sk in "skill", e.g. Ischia
z	at the beginning of a word like dz in "adze", otherwise like ts

An accent on an Italian word shows that the stress is on the last syllable.
In other cases we have shown which syllable is stressed by placing a dot below the relevant vowel.

IN BRIEF

Yes/No/Maybe	Sì/No/Forse
Please/Thank you	Per favore/Grazie
Excuse me, please!	Scusa!/Mi scusi
May I ...?/Pardon?	Posso ...? / Come dice?/Prego?
Good morning!/Good afternoon!/	Buon giorno!/Buon giorno!/
Good evening!/Good night!	Buona sera!/Buona notte!
Hello!/Goodbye!/See you	Ciao!/Salve! / Arrivederci!/Ciao!
My name is ...	Mi chiamo ...
What's your name?	Come si chiama?/Come ti chiami
I would like to .../Have you got ...?	Vorrei .../Avete ...?
How much is ...?	Quanto costa ...?
I (don't) like that	(Non) mi piace
good/bad	buono/cattivo
broken/doesn't work	guasto/non funziona
too much/much/little/all/nothing	troppo/molto/poco/ tutto/niente
Help!/Attention!/Caution!	aiuto!/attenzione!/prudenza!
ambulance/police/fire brigade	ambulanza/polizia/vigili del fuoco
Prohibition/forbidden	divieto/vietato
danger/dangerous	pericolo/pericoloso

DATE & TIME

Monday/Tuesday/Wednesday	lunedì/martedì/mercoledì
Thursday/Friday/Saturday	giovedì/venerdì/sabato

Parli italiano?

'Do you speak Italian?' This guide will help you to
say the basic words and phrases in Italian.

Sunday/holiday/working day	domenica/(giorno) festivo (giorno) feriale
today/tomorrow/yesterday	oggi/domani/ieri
hour/minute	ora/minuto
week/month/year	settimana/mese/anno
What time is it?	Che ora è? Che ore sono?
It's three o'clock/It's half past three	Sono le tre/Sono le tre e mezza
a quarter to four/ a quarter past four	le quattro meno un quarto/ un quarto alle quattro

TRAVEL

open/closed	aperto/chiuso
entrance/exit	entrata/uscita
departure/arrival	partenza/arrivo
toilets/ladies/gentlemen	bagno/signore/signori
(no) drinking water	acqua (non) potabile
Where is ...?/Where are ...?	Dov'è ...?/Dove sono ...?
left/right/straight ahead/back	sinistra/destra/dritto/indietro
close/far	vicino/lontano
bus/tram	bus/tram
taxi	taxi/tassì
bus stop/taxi stand	fermata/posteggio taxi
parking lot/parking garage	parcheggio/parcheggio coperto
street map/map	pianta/mappa
train station/harbour/airport	stazione/porto/aeroporto
schedule/ticket/supplement	orario/biglietto/supplemento
single/return	solo andata/andata e ritorno
train/track/platform	treno/binario/banchina
I would like to rent ...	Vorrei noleggiare ...
a car/a bicycle/boat	una macchina/una bicicletta/una barca
petrol/gas station	distributore/stazione di servizio
petrol/gas/diesel	benzina/diesel/gasolio
breakdown/repair shop	guasto/officina

FOOD & DRINK

Could you please book a table for tonight for four?	Vorrei prenotare per stasera un tavolo per quattro?
on the terrace/by the window	sulla terrazza/ vicino alla finestra
The menu, please	Il menù, per favore
bottle/carafe/glass	bottiglia/caraffa/bicchiere

knife/fork/spoon	coltello/forchetta/cucchiaio
salt/pepper/sugar	sale/pepe/ zucchero
vinegar/oil/milk/cream/lemon	aceto/olio/latte/panna/limone
cold/too salty/not cooked	freddo/troppo salato/non cotto
with/without ice/sparkling	con/senza ghiaccio/gas
vegetarian/allergy	vegetariano/vegetariana/allergia
May I have the bill, please?	Vorrei pagare/Il conto, per favore
bill/tip	conto/mancia

SHOPPING

Where can I find...?	Dove posso trovare ...?
I'd like .../I'm looking for ...	Vorrei .../Cerco ...
Do you put photos onto CD?	Vorrei masterizzare delle foto su CD?
pharmacy	farmacia
baker/market	forno/mercato
shopping centre/department store	centro commerciale/grande magazzino
grocery	negozio alimentare
supermarket	supermercato
photographic items/newspaper shop	articoli per foto/giornalaio
100 grammes/1 kilo	un etto/un chilo
expensive/cheap/price	caro/economico/prezzo
organically grown	di agricoltura biologica

ACCOMMODATION

Do you have any ... left?	Avete ancora ...
single room/double room	una (camera) singola/doppia
breakfast/half board/ full board	prima colazione/mezza pensione/
(American plan)	pensione completa
at the front/seafront/lakefront	con vista/con vista sul mare/lago
shower/sit-down bath/balcony/terrace	doccia/bagno/balcone/terrazza
key/room card	chiave/scheda magnetica
luggage/suitcase/bag	bagaglio/valigia/borsa

BANKS, MONEY & CREDIT CARDS

bank/ATM/pin code	banca/bancomat/ codice segreto
cash/credit card	in contanti/carta di credito
bill/coin/change	banconota/moneta/il resto

HEALTH

doctor/dentist/paediatrician	medico/dentista/pediatra
hospital/emergency clinic	ospedale/pronto soccorso
fever/pain	febbre/dolori

diarrhoea/nausea/sunburn	diarrea/nausea/scottatura solare
inflamed/injured	infiammato/ferito
plaster/bandage/ointment/cream	cerotto/fasciatura/pomata/crema
pain reliever/tablet/suppository	antidolorifico/compressa/supposta

TELECOMMUNICATIONS & MEDIA

stamp/letter/postcard	francobollo/lettera/cartolina
I need a landline phone card	Mi serve una scheda telefonica per la rete fissa
I'm looking for a prepaid card for my mobile	Cerco una scheda prepagata per il mio cellulare
Where can I find internet access?	Dove trovo un accesso internet?
dial/connection/engaged	comporre/linea/occupato
socket/adapter/charger	presa/riduttore/caricabatterie
computer/battery/rechargeable battery	computer/batteria/accumulatore
"at" (@) sign	chiocciola
internet address (URL)/e-mail address	indirizzo internet/indirizzo email
internet connection/wifi	collegamento internet/wi-fi
e-mail/file/print	email/file/stampare

LEISURE, SPORTS & BEACH

beach/bathing beach	spiaggia/bagno/stabilimento balneare
sunshade/lounger	ombrellone/sdraio/funivia
(rescue) hut/avalanche	rifugio/valanga
cable car/chair lift	funivia/seggiovia

NUMBERS

0	zero	17	diciassette
1	uno	18	diciotto
2	due	19	diciannove
3	tre	20	venti
4	quattro	21	ventuno
5	cinque	30	trenta
6	sei	40	quaranta
7	sette	50	cinquanta
8	otto	60	sessanta
9	nove	70	settanta
10	dieci	80	ottanta
11	undici	90	novanta
12	dodici	100	cento
13	tredici	1000	mille
14	quattordici	2000	duemila
15	quindici	½	un mezzo
16	sedici	¼	un quarto

ROAD ATLAS

The green line indicates the Discovery Tour "Lake Garda at a glance"
The blue line indicates the other Discovery Tours

All tours are also marked on the pull-out map

Photo: Torbole

Exploring Lake Garda

The map on the back cover shows how
the area has been sub-divided

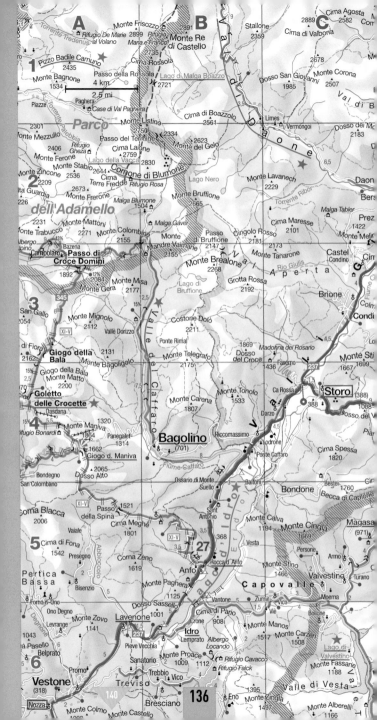

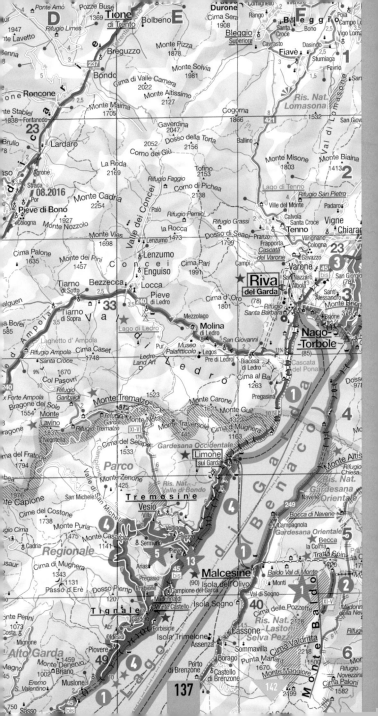

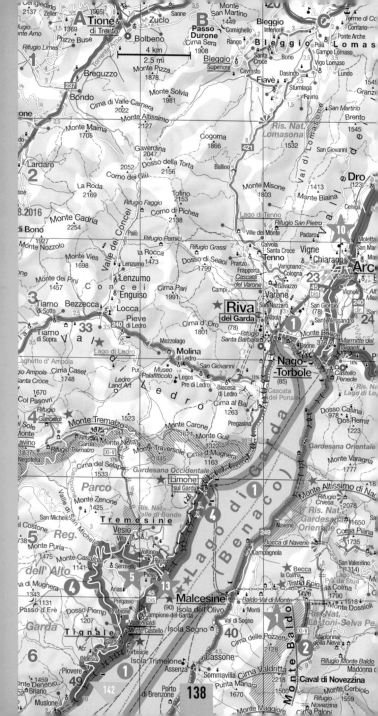

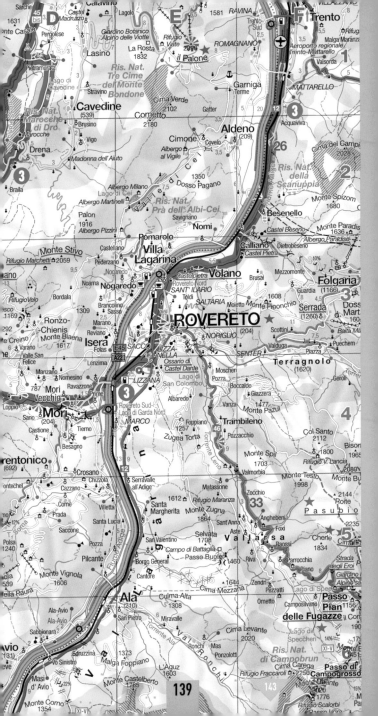

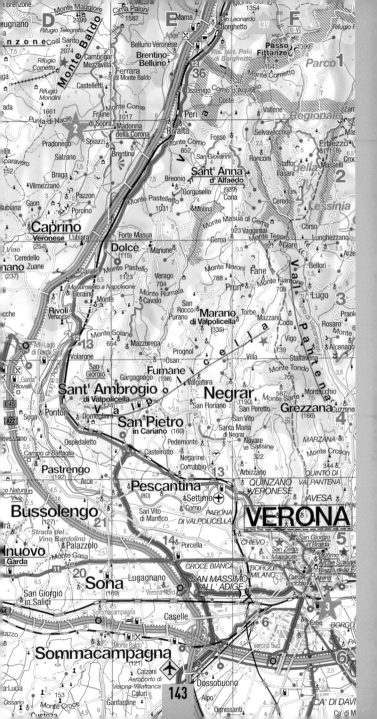

KEY TO ROAD ATLAS

Autobahn · Gebührenpflichtige Anschlussstelle · Gebührenstelle · Anschlussstelle mit Nummer · Rasthaus mit Übernachtung · Raststätte · Kleinraststätte · Tankstelle · Parkplatz mit und ohne WC	Trento 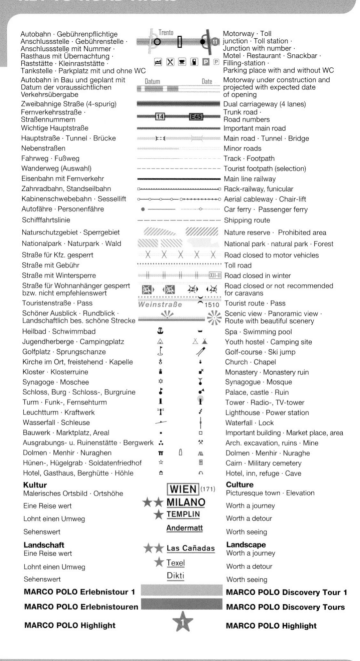 11	Motorway · Toll junction · Toll station · Junction with number · Motel · Restaurant · Snackbar · Filling-station · Parking place with and without WC
Autobahn in Bau und geplant mit Datum der voraussichtlichen Verkehrsübergabe	Datum — Date	Motorway under construction and projected with expected date of opening
Zweibahnige Straße (4-spurig)		Dual carriageway (4 lanes)
Fernverkehrsstraße · Straßennummern	14 E45	Trunk road · Road numbers
Wichtige Hauptstraße		Important main road
Hauptstraße · Tunnel · Brücke	)=(	Main road · Tunnel · Bridge
Nebenstraßen		Minor roads
Fahrweg · Fußweg		Track · Footpath
Wanderweg (Auswahl)		Tourist footpath (selection)
Eisenbahn mit Fernverkehr		Main line railway
Zahnradbahn, Standseilbahn		Rack-railway, funicular
Kabinenschwebebahn · Sessellift		Aerial cableway · Chair-lift
Autofähre · Personenfähre	● ○	Car ferry · Passenger ferry
Schifffahrtslinie		Shipping route
Naturschutzgebiet · Sperrgebiet		Nature reserve · Prohibited area
Nationalpark · Naturpark · Wald		National park · natural park · Forest
Straße für Kfz. gesperrt	X X X X X	Road closed to motor vehicles
Straße mit Gebühr		Toll road
Straße mit Wintersperre	XII-II	Road closed in winter
Straße für Wohnanhänger gesperrt bzw. nicht empfehlenswert		Road closed or not recommended for caravans
Touristenstraße · Pass	Weinstraße 1510	Tourist route · Pass
Schöner Ausblick · Rundblick · Landschaftlich bes. schöne Strecke		Scenic view · Panoramic view · Route with beautiful scenery
Heilbad · Schwimmbad		Spa · Swimming pool
Jugendherberge · Campingplatz	△ X A	Youth hostel · Camping site
Golfplatz · Sprungschanze		Golf-course · Ski jump
Kirche im Ort, freistehend · Kapelle		Church · Chapel
Kloster · Klosterruine		Monastery · Monastery ruin
Synagoge · Moschee		Synagogue · Mosque
Schloss, Burg · Schloss-, Burgruine		Palace, castle · Ruin
Turm · Funk-, Fernsehturm		Tower · Radio-, TV-tower
Leuchtturm · Kraftwerk		Lighthouse · Power station
Wasserfall · Schleuse		Waterfall · Lock
Bauwerk · Marktplatz, Areal		Important building · Market place, area
Ausgrabungs- u. Ruinenstätte · Bergwerk		Arch. excavation, ruins · Mine
Dolmen · Menhir · Nuraghen	π ∩ ᴧ	Dolmen · Menhir · Nuraghe
Hünen-, Hügelgrab · Soldatenfriedhof	☆ ⊞	Cairn · Military cemetery
Hotel, Gasthaus, Berghütte · Höhle	☖ ∩	Hotel, inn, refuge · Cave

Kultur — Culture

Malerisches Ortsbild · Ortshöhe	WIEN (171)	Picturesque town · Elevation
Eine Reise wert	★★ MILANO	Worth a journey
Lohnt einen Umweg	★ TEMPLIN	Worth a detour
Sehenswert	Andermatt	Worth seeing

Landschaft — Landscape

Eine Reise wert	★★ Las Cañadas	Worth a journey
Lohnt einen Umweg	★ Texel	Worth a detour
Sehenswert	Dikti	Worth seeing

MARCO POLO Erlebnistour 1		MARCO POLO Discovery Tour 1
MARCO POLO Erlebnistouren		MARCO POLO Discovery Tours
MARCO POLO Highlight	★ 1	MARCO POLO Highlight

MARCO POLO TRAVEL GUIDES

Algarve
Amsterdam
Andalucia
Athens
Australia
Austria
Bali & Lombok
Bangkok
Barcelona
Berlin
Brazil
Bruges
Brussels
Budapest
Bulgaria
California
Cambodia
Canada East
Canada West / Rockies
& Vancouver
Cape Town &
Garden Route
Cape Verde
Channel Islands
Chicago & The Lakes
China
Cologne
Copenhagen
Corfu
Costa Blanca
& Valencia
Costa Brava
Costa del Sol & Granada
Crete
Cuba
Cyprus (North and
South)
Devon & Cornwall
Dresden
Dubai

Dublin
Dubrovnik &
Dalmatian Coast
Edinburgh
Egypt
Egypt Red Sea Resorts
Finland
Florence
Florida
French Atlantic Coast
French Riviera
(Nice, Cannes & Monaco)
Fuerteventura
Gran Canaria
Greece
Hamburg
Hong Kong & Macau
Iceland
India
India South
Ireland
Israel
Istanbul
Italy
Japan
Jordan
Kos
Krakow
Lake Garda
Lanzarote
Las Vegas
Lisbon
London
Los Angeles
Madeira & Porto Santo
Madrid
Mallorca
Malta & Gozo
Mauritius
Menorca

Milan
Montenegro
Morocco
Munich
Naples & Amalfi Coast
New York
New Zealand
Norway
Oslo
Oxford
Paris
Peru & Bolivia
Phuket
Portugal
Prague
Rhodes
Rome
Salzburg
San Francisco
Santorini
Sardinia
Scotland
Seychelles
Shanghai
Sicily
Singapore
South Africa
Sri Lanka
Stockholm
Switzerland
Tenerife
Thailand
Turkey
Turkey South Coast
Tuscany
United Arab Emirates
USA Southwest
(Las Vegas, Colorado,
New Mexico, Arizona
& Utah)
Venice
Vienna
Vietnam
Zakynthos & Ithaca,
Kefalonia, Lefkas

The travel guides with
Insider
Tips

INDEX

This index lists all places, beaches and destinations featured in this guide. Numbers in bold indicate a main entry.

WRITE TO US

e-mail: info@marcopologuides.co.uk
Did you have a great holiday?
Is there something on your mind?
Whatever it is, let us know!
Whether you want to praise, alert us
to errors or give us a personal tip –
MARCO POLO would be pleased to
hear from you.
We do everything we can to provide the
very latest information for your trip.

Nevertheless, despite all of our authors'
thorough research, errors can creep in.
MARCO POLO does not accept any
liability for this. Please contact us by
e-mail or post.
MARCO POLO Travel Publishing Ltd
Pinewood, Chineham Business Park
Crockford Lane, Chineham
Basingstoke, Hampshire RG24 8AL
United Kingdom

PICTURE CREDITS
Cover photograph: Getty Images: A. Talán
Photos: DuMont Bildarchiv: Bernhart (flap left, 120/121, 122 o.), Mosler (55, 123); S. Engelhardt (1 below); © fotolia.com: rcaucino (18 top); Getty Images: E. Marongiu (19 below), A. Talán (1), F. Vallenari (22/23); Getty Images/Kontributor: F. Bienewald (31); huber-images: U. Bernhart (25), F. Cogoli (76), Friedel (116/117), Gräfenhain (34, 77, 134/135), Huber (4 top, 64, 86), H.-P. Huber (12/13), J. Huber (45), H. Klaes (63), K. Kreder (96/97), S. Raccanello (5, 29); Laif: F. Blickle (11), Bungert (flap right), Celentano (28 right), M. Galli (17, 75); T. Gerber (37, 98), Gollhardt/Wieland (89), G. Heidorn (48), Kreuels (120), B. Steinhilber (80/81, 106/107), C. Zahn (92), H. D. Zinn (6); Laif/Le Figaro Magazine: Sander (30/31); Look: I. Pompe (8, 19 top, 40), A. Strauß (7), H. Wohrer (60/61); mauritius images/imagebroker (109), S. Lubenow (39), A. Reinert (85), Siepmann (102); mauritius images/Tetra Images/Tetra Images (18 below); mauritius images: U. Bernhart (70/71, 94), R. Kaessmann (32/33), B. Kickner (4 below, 112/113), P. Lehner (2, 47), M. Pinn (78), M. Zirn (3); mauritius images/Alamy (9, 72, 110, 121), MARKA (52, 82); mauritius images/CuboImages (118); mauritius images/foodcollection (26/27); mauritius images/STOCK4B-RF (18 centre); mauritius images/Travel Collection: T. Langlotz (20/21, 42, 66, 90, 108); O. Stadler (58, 68, 122 below); T. Stankiewicz (14/15, 30, 50/51, 57, 115); vario images/imagebroker (10); vario images/Westend61 (28 left)

3rd edition – fully revised and updated 2018
Worldwide Distribution: Marco Polo Travel Publishing Ltd., Pinewood; Chineham Business Park, Crockford Lane, Basingstoke, Hampshire RG24 8AL, UK. Email: sales@marcopolouk.com
© MAIRDUMONT GmbH & Co. KG, Ostfildern
Chief editor: Marion Zorn
Author: Barbara Schaefer, Co-author: Saskia Engelhardt; editor: Nikolai Michaelis
Programme supervision: Lucas Forst-Gill, Susanne Heimburger, Johanna Jiranek, Nikolai Michaelis, Kristin Wittemann
Picture editor: Gabriele Forst, Stefanie Wiese; What's hot: Saskia Engelhardt, wunder media, München
Cartography road atlas and pull-out map: © MAIRDUMONT, Ostfildern
Cover design, p. 1, pull-out map cover: Karl Anders – Büro für Visual Stories, Hamburg; design inside: milchhof: atelier, Berlin; design p. 2/3, Discovery Tours: Susan Chaaban Dipl.-Des. (FH)
Translated from German by Christopher Wynne, Jennifer Walcoff Neuheiser and Suzanne Kirkbright
Editorial office: SAW Communications, Redaktionsbüro Dr. Sabine A. Werner, Mainz: Frauke Feuchter, Julia Gilcher, Cosima Talhouni, Dr. Sabine A. Werner; prepress: SAW Communications, Mainz, in cooperation with alles hat Medien, Mainz
Phrase book in cooperation with Ernst Klett Sprachen GmbH, Stuttgart,
Editorial by Pons Wörterbücher

MIX
Paper from
responsible sources
FSC® C124385
www.fsc.org

DOS & DON'TS

A few things you should avoid doing

GO EVERYWHERE BY CAR

A quick trip to Limone, an afternoon in Malcesine, a swim in Sirmione – but are you sure you want to go by car and leave your (usually free) hotel parking space? Take the boat for a change! You won't get stuck in a traffic jam and won't have to look for an expensive parking place.

TAKE THE CABLE CAR UP MONTE BALDO IN AUGUST

The same holds true for any sunny summer days, holidays or long weekends. If you don't manage to catch the first car up, you might end up queuing for ages. Not to mention, once you're at the top, you also have to wait forever to go back down!

BELIEVE THE FORECAST

Don't be discouraged by predications of bad weather. The close proximity to glaciers and the Po River valley make an accurate forecast difficult. Most of the time, it's better than expected.

INAPPROPRIATE CLOTHING

Where tourists drag themselves through the narrow streets of Old Towns in shorts, shirts and sandals, the fashionable Italian woman even wears high heels in difficult terrain (cobblestones). You don't have to go as far, but sitting down at a café table in bathing shorts is really a faux pas.

ORDER IN ENGLISH

Of course, most Lake Garda waiters will understand you when you order "a beer". But, how about learning a handful of Italian words? Drawing the waiter's attention with a polite *scusi* – excuse me – is almost certain to lead to success.

TRAVEL FROM LAZISE TO PESCHIERA ON A SATURDAY AFTERNOON

The road passes the major leisure parks and when the masses flood out of these the roads become hopelessly jammed. Just as important: if you want to visit one of these parks, don't do it at the weekend. You will simply be pushed through – especially in August.

FERRAGOSTO ON LAGO DI GARDA

If at all possible, do not travel to Lake Garda around 15 August! That is when all of Italy is on holiday and the traffic comes to a standstill. It is usually just as packed on the beaches around the lake.

BUYING COUNTERFEIT GOODS

Beware of alleged top offers! Selling as well as buying counterfeit branded clothes and faked branded bags is punished with high fines. This applies to foreign tourists, too.